WORKING WITHOUT A NET

WORKING WITHOUT A NET

How to Survive & Thrive in Today's High Risk Business World

MORRIS R. SHECHTMAN

PRENTICE HALL
Englewood Cliffs, New Jersey 07632

Prentice-Hall International (UK) Limited, London
Prentice-Hall of Australia Pty. Limited, Sydney
Prentice-Hall Canada, Inc., Toronto
Prentice-Hall Hispanoamericana, S.A., Mexico
Prentice-Hall of India Private Limited, New Delhi
Prentice-Hall of Japan, Inc., Tokyo
Simon & Schuster Asia Pte. Ltd., Singapore
Editora Prentice-Hall do Brasil, Ltda., Rio de Janeiro

©1994 by
PRENTICE HALL, Inc.
Englewood Cliffs, NJ

10   9   8   7   6   5   4

Library of Congress Cataloging-in-Publication Data

Shechtman, Morris R.
  Working without a net: how to survive & thrive in today's high risk
business world/Morris R. Shechtman.
    p.   cm.
  ISBN 0-13-026239-0
  1. Personal management. 2. Organizational change. 3. Success in business. 4. Risk management. I. Title
650.14--dc20   94-29919
                                                                      CIP

ISBN 0-13-026239-0

PRENTICE HALL
Career and Personal Development
Englewood Cliffs, NJ 07632

Simon & Schuster, A Paramount Communications Company

Printed in the United States of America

DEDICATION

This book is dedicated to two people:

My father, Dr. Charles Shechtman, who exemplified commitment and value integrity in everything he did. His death, during the writing of this book, has left an irreparable hole in my life.

And my wife, Arleah, who has taught me, over the past seventeen years, what growth, challenge, and joy are really about.

CONTENTS

CHAPTER 3

THE IMPACT OF INFORMATION ON COMPETITIVE ADVANTAGE   35

CHAPTER 6
THE HIGH RISK CULTURE   79

PART TWO: GROWTH AND SUCCESS   89

CHAPTER 7
GROWTH AND SUCCESS: HIGH RISK MODELS AND TOOLS   91

CHAPTER 8

INDIVIDUAL GROWTH AND SUCCESS: LEARNING TO COPE WITH LOSS   103

CHAPTER 9

SUCCESS AND GROWTH AS A GRIEVING PROCESS   113

CHAPTER 16

LOYALTY IN A HIGH RISK CULTURE   207

PART FIVE: AUTONOMY, STRUCTURE, AND ETHICS   215

CHAPTER 17

AUTONOMY AND INDEPENDENCE   217

PREFACE

"I can't deal with all the changes going on in my office."

"I don't know how I can balance the needs of my family with all the extra work my job demands."

"There's no loyalty here any more; this company isn't the same one I joined seven years ago."

These statements can be heard in the lunchrooms and boardrooms of every organization. Junior executives make them; so do CEOs. People are acutely aware that things have changed and are continuing, to change, and they're having difficulty handling it. It's not just that they're unhappy. It's that they're unproductive and stagnant. Their personal lives are being affected by what's going on at work. They're unable to put themselves or their organizations in a growth mode, and they don't know what to do about it.

This book will suggest what to do. Its premise is that all the rules have changed, and we need to start learning the new rules. For some this might be a radical premise. It's uncomfortable to realize that we can no longer run our businesses on the old assumptions:

- Expecting blind loyalty from our people in exchange for job security.

- Delaying decisions for days, weeks, months, or years.

- Accepting mediocre job performance.

- Embracing consensus and avoiding conflict.

In the following pages, I'll discuss these and other assumptions that are no longer valid and introduce you to the new assumptions—or paradigms—that govern our world. You'll find ideas, techniques, and tools that will help you survive and thrive in this new high risk business world.

If you doubt that you, your people, or your organization are capable of adapting to this new environment, let me preview one critical paradigm. Rather than accepting the fatalistic notion that some of us are too old or set in our ways to change, this paradigm embodies the optimistics free-will spirit of this book: *People's ability to change is not a function of capacity but of choice.*

Morris Shechtman

PART ONE
SURVIVING THE HIGH RISK CULTURE

C H A P T E R
AN ALTERNATIVE TO WORKING AND LIVING IN A FANTASY WORLD

Denial is crippling American business.

Companies can lose phenomenal sums of money for months and deny that anything is amiss, until losses are too large to be ignored. Then they swing the downsizing meat cleaver in a futile attempt to cut their losses. This has happened at General Motors, at most of the airlines, at IBM—the list goes on and on. When asked why they didn't do anything about their mounting losses earlier, these companies respond, "We were waiting for it to turn around," or "We can't do much about it because we can't get the labor force to cooperate." These excuses are nothing more than denials that the situation is bad and must be changed.

Denial also takes place on an individual level. Some chronically unemployed people would find jobs quickly if they would stop pretending that their industry is still alive and well or that they can find work in the city in which they've always lived. The decline of certain industries mandates that people consider other types of employers; when jobs dry up in a city or town, it is time to look for work elsewhere. Yet how many people even now are denying what is plainly obvious?

Denial isn't limited to the chronically unemployed. It can be seen in CEOs as well as junior-level executives. Managers, for instance, frequently tolerate behavior in subordinates that can only be described as bizarre; they see their people having serious problems, yet they fail to take action that will force people to resolve problems. A client recently told me that one of her employees didn't show up at work for a week because, the employee said, her husband and kids were killed in a car accident. My client did some checking and learned that the woman had been divorced years ago and didn't have any kids. It turns out that this was only one of many stories this person made up when she missed work.

I asked my client what she was doing about this person. "Nothing," she told me, "except we did tell her that her behavior was kind of strange."

Why did she deny that her employee was acting a few bricks shy of a load? Because she, like many managers, didn't want to confront her subordinate. She was afraid of conflict and assumed it would destroy the relationship. She also seemed to be afraid of the self-examination such a confrontation might produce, about what it might reveal about her own life.

Many people today feel beaten down by the rapid pace of change in their personal and professional lives, yet rather than attempt to deal with change, they deny it. This decision to avoid the reality of change is the catalyst for this book. During my consulting work, I've been astonished and dismayed observing the toll denial has taken on the business world and on ourselves.

KEEPING THE SAFETY NETS IN PLACE

What feeds this denial is a compulsion to reproduce the familiar in our lives. People are afraid of conflict and change, of things that are new or different. They maintain their familiar cocoons at all costs—even at the cost of their jobs, their families and even their lives. An employee who was verbally abused as a child finds a boss whose refrain to that employee is, "I really should get rid of you, but at least you work cheap."

This drive to reproduce the familiar is much stronger than the drive to produce what is healthy. It is why some people stay in relationships where they're emotionally or physically abused—the abuse might not be healthy, but it is familiar.

Here's another example of how the familiar is reproduced in organizations. Certain managers surround themselves with inept or marginal subordinates. These managers complain about their subordinates daily, moaning about how difficult they are to deal with. Yet despite all this moaning and groaning, managers maintain the status quo. What they're really doing is maintaining their early family structure. Employees take the place of siblings and mom and dad—they've duplicated that same dysfunctional family unit. "Joe is always getting in these silly, unproductive competitions with Jim," one manager might say, simultaneously describing arguments between two subordinates and his family's sibling rivalry. This manager isn't overly concerned if his people work productively, only that they provide him with a certain level of emotional familiarity. In the past, managers like this kept their jobs for year after year because the business culture maintained safety nets. For example, denial is a big safety net for a poor performer, like this manager. His boss denied the problem or made more excuses, so the manager wasn't held accountable for performance. Confronting this manager about his group's productivity would be stressful. Firing him would make other managers uncomfortable. Everyone looked the other way.

WHY IT DOESN'T WORK ANYMORE

Denial has been part of human nature since there have been humans. People have stumbled through their personal and professional lives, replaying old tapes, always seeking the familiar. Somehow, we've gotten this far.

However, forces are reshaping the way humans live and work together. We are at the threshold of a time in which we can no longer survive in a state of denial. The rapid rate of social, cultural, political, and economic change in the world today has created what I call the *high risk culture*. In this culture our businesses and our lives are in a constant state of flux, and there is no room for safety nets. To succeed in such a culture, we must learn to work with change, not deny it. And with our safety nets gone and our external props kicked away, we must learn to work together in new ways while we find sources of stability within ourselves.

The time has come to insist on peak productivity, from ourselves and from our employers, employees, and coworkers. Any business trying to succeed in a high risk culture is like a troupe of circus acrobats—every individual must be counted on to do his or her part to keep the act in motion. If the performers don't interconnect, the results can be fatal—especially when there's only air separating the performers from the ground.

A GREAT CAPACITY FOR CHANGE

The high risk culture seems to be a frightening place, but it doesn't have to be. This book's theme is highly optimistic: People and organizations are capable of great change. The information, tools, and exercises provided here are designed to facilitate those changes. Contrary to a common distortion of Freudian thinking, people aren't set in stone at the age of five. To change and grow is possible for anyone, as long as he or she is ambitious and can sustain the discomfort that is part of the process.

Learning to work without a net makes discomfort tolerable. Working without a net doesn't mean taking crazy risks. It means becoming less reliant on traditional symbols of security such as one particular job (that you've done for years but offers no growth or challenge) or a town (where you've lived all your life simply because it's familiar). In effect, we exchange our external nets for internal ones. Internal security nets are portable. When we take a new job or take on a new challenge, our inner strengths travel with us. That internal security gives us the confidence to evolve and grow without panic or remorse.

BENEFITS OF WORKING WITHOUT A NET

Up to this point, I've introduced some elements of the theory behind this book. But this is not a theoretical or an academic book. Its concepts can be and have been applied successfully by thousands of individuals and organizations. Although there are numerous applications, let's focus on some of the more critical ones:

- **Job marketability**. No matter what happens—from acquisitions to downturns—you'll realize that you can make the transition to whatever the new reality becomes. Developing that portable sense of security will be explained in detail. Just as important, you will learn the two skills that will greatly increase your value to organizations: decision-making and relationship-building. Instead of presenting yourself to prospective employers as someone looking for a job, you can demonstrate that you possess the skills to increase the organization's profits in a high-risk culture.

- **Hiring**. Managers will be able to differentiate between growth-oriented and comfort-oriented people in the hiring process. With the former, a lengthy internship or training period is unnecessary. Growth-oriented people have a very fast learning curve and are much less likely to leave a high-risk organization (thus reducing turnover). By helping you identify growth-oriented people, I'll help you avoid hiring people with value systems that are mismatched to the organization.

- **Competitive advantage**. Many of my clients use the high-risk approach to adapt to changes in the economy and marketplace faster than competitors. They can react swiftly and decisively to new trends, and they don't panic and assume a crisis mentality when a sudden shift occurs. The ability to respond quickly and effectively to change is critical for success in a high-risk culture.

- **Personal payoff**. Relationship-building skills aren't limited to work environments. The skills offered here will be useful in establishing stronger relationships with spouses, children, and other important people. How to build a truly reciprocal relationship early on and avoid divorce or codependent relationships down the road will be discussed. I'll also help readers capitalize on the connection between personal and professional relationships—the realization that poor personal relationships affect professional performance negatively (and vice versa) and that restructuring one area of life positively affects the other.

HOW I KNOW WHAT I KNOW

The concepts presented in this book are a result of many experiences in three different careers. I'd like to give you a sense of a few of those experiences and how they came to shape my philosophy.

Years ago, as a university professor, I watched students go through class after class without any understanding of the process with which they were involved. Without any real-life experience, their orientation was toward comfort: a drive to get to a place where there is a cessation of demands. Most of them never had the chance to put information to use in any meaningful way outside of a classroom. Any information that made them uncomfortable—that demanded growth from them—was tuned out. Most of them turned in mediocre performances as a result of this drive toward comfort. Success was possible only for those students who had sufficient life experience to endure the discomfort that comes with growth.

Later, as a psychotherapist, I encountered patients searching for direction and a way of viewing the world. People would come in with problems related to change, desperate to know if a course of action should be pursued, whether it was right or wrong. Patients would relate the counterproductive things they had done, the result of reproducing destructive, familiar patterns in their lives. They wanted and needed a sorting mechanism so they could evaluate their actions within a coherent context.

The sorting mechanism that was most helpful to them was a clear value orientation. When they understood their core beliefs, my patients had a way to judge what was stupid, destructive behavior and what was not. Unfortunately, therapists are trained to be value neutral and simply tell patients to "take a look at that." After patients take a look, they have no idea what to do next.

From these experiences, I realized that people are hungry for values; that they flounder without values to guide their behavior. A value-based life, it seemed to me, would be a highly productive, satisfying one. It would provide the internal sense of security necessary to deal with a rapidly changing world.

As a business consultant, I discovered that organizations also lack values. They don't possess core belief systems (a collection of values). They manage their companies based on what works at the moment and what keeps them in familiar territory; they are prey for trends and fads. As a result, they ride the rollercoaster cycle of good results and bad results, puzzled by their inconsistency.

For instance, most organizations rarely define the role of management beyond processing paper and "watching" people. Although management may say it wants to foster growth among its employees, its actions often belie that statement. To truly foster growth, management must act as a change agent, and if it doesn't take on this role, it's being paid too much. When this value of growth is missing from organizations, the majority of employees plateau in their careers; there is no impetus from management for them to achieve new and more challenging objectives.

When management acts as a change agent, it confronts accountability issues. Think about how many times a boss tells subordinates, "You're grown-ups here, not children. I expect you to be accountable for the tasks you've been assigned." He or she expects them to be accountable to themselves, which is impossible. Accountability doesn't exist outside of relationships. You have to be accountable to someone else. Management must assign someone for a subordinate to be accountable to; that's the only way the subordinate will grow. An apt analogy is to a family. We don't throw our kids out on the street at an early age and expect them to grow (emotionally and intellectually) on their own; we don't give them complete freedom and no limits. We manage our relationships with kids. Why should we abdicate our responsibility to manage employee relationships?

What are your values? Your company's values? To help you determine your values and see how they fit within the high risk culture, take the time to complete the Value Clarification Instrument on pages 10-12. Save the answer sheet for later. In Chapter 9, I'll help you evaluate your responses and understand where you reside on the risk continuum. I'd like you to complete this exercise now rather than later because the information in the following chapters might influence your answers.

Value Clarification Instrument

Choose statement A, B, or C as the one that best reflects your feelings and values. Please circle only one response (A, B, or C) under each item.

1A.   A job is a privilege extended to an employee, by an employer.

1B.   A job is an inherent right guaranteed by society.

1C.   I feel equally divided between response A and response B.

2A.   People begin to change when they feel comfortable, supported and positively reinforced.

2B.   People begin to change when they become more uncomfortable than comfortable with their current circumstances.

2C.   I feel equally divided between response A and response B.

3A.   Security is best defined through tangible things - living in one place for an extended period of time, job security, having the same friends.

3B.   Security is best defined through factors that are primarily internal - certainty about one's marketability in different settings and jobs; the knowledge that you can meet your personal and professional needs.

3C.   I feel equally divided between response A and response B.

4A.   Failure is as important to the learning process as success; try and minimize failure and you decrease your capacity to learn.

4B.   People learn best through successful experiences; try and maximize success and eliminate failure.

4C.   I feel equally divided between response A and response B.

5A.   Homelessness and other related problems are social problems; they reflect a society's inability to deal effectively with social issues.

5B.   With the exception of a small number of defined populations, homelessness and other related problems are not social problems; they are expressions of individual choice.

5C.   I feel equally divided between response A and response B.

Value
Clarification
Instrument *(Cont'd)...*

6A.   Confrontation and conflict are two types of problem-solving strategies - everyone can use them effectively.

6B.   Confrontation and conflict are last-resort strategies, and they often make matters worse.

6C.   I feel equally divided between response A and response B.

7A.   An employee's personal problems are none of an employer's business as long as the employee is currently doing his/her job adequately.

7B.   Sooner or later, personal problems aggravate work problems, and vice versa. Employers have an obligation to employees to hold them accountable for developing plans designed to resolve personal problems which have the potential to affect work performance.

7C.   I feel equally divided between response A and response B.

8A.   Both money earned **and** impact created in one's job are necessary measures of success in one's work.

8B.   Either money earned **or** impact created in one's job is a valid measure of success in one's work.

8C.   I feel equally divided between response A and response B.

9A.   The best personal relationships are based upon common interests, activities and backgrounds.

9B.   The best personal relationships are based upon each person's demand for personal growth from oneself and the other person.

9C.   I feel equally divided between response A and response B.

10A.   Many people have two or three strikes against them from the start and often end up as victims through no fault of their own.

10B.   With the exception of physical or mental handicaps, adults are never victims, they create their own problems and can create their own solutions.

10C.   I feel equally divided between response A and response B.

Value
Clarification
Instrument *(Cont'd)...*

Answer Sheet

Circle the letter that most closely matches your position on each
of the 10 items. You can circle only one letter for each value
continuum. Do not make any marks in between any of the letters.

1.   A   C   B

2.   A   C   B

3.   A   C   B

4.   A   C   B

5.   A   C   B

6.   A   C   B

7.   A   C   B

8.   A   C   B

9.   A   C   B

10.   A   C   B

A CARING APPROACH

Managing relationships frequently involves what some people might perceive to be difficult situations. Conflict and confrontation are part of the process, and many executives try to avoid these seemingly unpleasant encounters. But conflict and confrontation don't have to involve hostility or personal attacks. Pointing out the flaws in someone's work performance or discussing a personal issue that is causing an employee to be consistently late for work doesn't require a patronizing lecture or a shouting match. When conflict and confrontation are part of a caring approach, managers don't have problems using these tools to help their people grow.

In fact, an uncaring approach avoids conflict and confrontation. What else would you call ignoring someone's barely passable work or counterproductive behavior? The message sent by such apathy is, "I don't really care enough to help you be more than mediocre."

The more we care, the more we should demand. Granted, it is easy for people to mistake our motivation when we demand growth. When we say, "Look, you've established one type of customer relationship over the years, and that has to change or you won't be adding value to the company," an employee can jump to the conclusion that we're being hostile or mean; that we're trying to *boss him around* or *control him*. Not at all. Change and growth entail some discomfort— no one enjoys being told that he or she is slacking off and that it won't be tolerated. But discomfort is part of the growth process, and it is impossible to get to the next level of development without it.

Let's return to our children analogy for a moment. When our kids start learning how to walk, they invariably bump into objects and fall down; they scream and cry in frustration. Should we as parents prevent this discomfort by picking them up and carrying them around? Is it a caring gesture to delay this natural and productive stage of growth?

Of course not. The more growth we facilitate, the more we care.

HOW THIS BOOK WILL FACILITATE YOUR ABILITY TO GROW AND MANAGE GROWTH

Part One, Chapters 2 through 6, will give you a sense of the enormous changes occurring in our high risk culture and how these changes affect us personally and professionally. Part One will provide you with the two skills essential to surviving and thriving in this culture: decision-making and relationship-building.

Part Two, Chapters 7 through 9, focuses on growth and success. In a high risk culture, individual and organizational growth and success can't be taken for granted. We need to develop an appropriate organizational model for rapidly expanding, high risk companies and deal with the losses that accompany growth and success. The material in Part Two will suggest ways and tools for doing so.

In Part Three, Chapters 10 through 13, I'll discuss the most common obstacles to growth and success that people in high risk cultures face. These obstacles—which include muddled values, adolescent-acting employees, perfunctory goal setting and the lack of accountability—can be overcome, and in Part Three we'll learn how.

Part Four, Chapters 14 through 16, revolves around an issue that needs to be viewed in a new light: how to manage conflict, anger and loyalty in a high risk culture. The traditional notions about how to deal with this issue no longer apply. I'll delve into new definitions of these terms and new ways of applying them productively and profitably.

Part Five, Chapters 17 through 19, deals with the growing interdependence of individuals, companies, and countries. The concept of the ruggedly independent American flies in the face of 1990s realities. I'll explore how autonomy, structure and ethics can help us live and work productively in an interdependent world.

AN ALTERNATIVE TO THE TYPICAL MANAGEMENT BOOK

In the following pages, you'll find concepts and models that are very different from what you've heard before; you've probably already sensed that from what you've read so far. My emphasis on the personal *and* the professional, the encouragement of confrontation and conflict, the need to deal with organizational denial—all this is light-years removed from the usual stuff about leadership and empowerment.

The traditional approaches aren't working. The losses suffered by our major corporations are monumental and intolerable. We are doing a poor job of handling change, and because the pace of change is accelerating, we won't survive without new change management skills.

The rules by which we run our lives and our businesses have changed. In the following chapters, I'll tell you what the new rules are and what every organization and individual can do to take advantage of them.

CHAPTER

SIX PARADIGMS FOR KEEPING YOUR BALANCE IN A HIGH RISK CULTURE

As we learned in Chapter 1, the safety nets of the old business culture are going or already gone. Other changes are taking place as well, changes that could cause you and your company to take a hard fall if you aren't prepared for them.

You've heard quality gurus use the term *paradigm shift* to describe the movement in manufacturing from mass production to lean production. *Paradigms* are defining rules or models, and they can be internal or external. Although the production example is a highly visible external shift, there are less visible but no less important internal paradigm shifts taking place. Awareness of these shifts is essential for those working without a net. Without that awareness, success and happiness in a high risk culture—a culture characterized by uncertainty, unpredictability, and rapid change—is impossible.

Unfortunately, internal paradigms aren't grasped as easily as a redesigned production process. Because they are intangible and so different from the paradigms they're replacing, it's easy not to notice them. But as you'll see, they are not only real, but individuals and organizations are already feeling their impact. When individuals capitalize on them, they are on the cutting edge of personal and professional growth and development. When organizations take advantage of them, they gain a competitive edge in the marketplace.

The six paradigm shifts affecting the business world today are as follows:

1. Caring for people is not synonymous with taking care of people.
2. People's ability to change is not a function of capacity but of choice.
3. We need to change out attitudes toward change.
4. We must redefine what constitutes *acceptable work*, moving from adequacy to peak performance.
5. Who we are personally is inextricably connected to who we are professionally; the goal is to lead *blended*, not *balanced*, lives.
6. We must create value-driven personal and professional lives.

Throughout this book, I will be referring back to these paradigms, pointing to their impact and showing how to work with them in your professional and personal life.

PARADIGM 1: Caring for people is not synonymous with taking care of people.

Families, government, and businesses have disabled people in the name of caring for them. Well-meaning policies have resulted in codependency, unemployment, and bankruptcy. Many apparently good intentions are undone by the confusion between *caretaking* and *caring for*.

Caretaking means that

• You do things for people that they're perfectly capable of doing for themselves.
• The things you do persuade people that they are unable to solve their own problems; that anyone else would be better able to solve them.

Caring for means that

• You challenge people to be the best they can be.
• You tell them what they need to hear, not what they want to hear.

Caretaking has been the accepted mode of management for many years. It encourages overachieving: A relatively small group of people are responsible for a relatively large amount of productive capacity. A few overextenders—overworked, highly committed employees—in a company carry the load, working nonstop to bring in business and get things done. In the past, it was possible for a business to get a free ride on a caretaker's back. Today, however, that caretaker will burn out. Too many opportunities and too much competition overwhelm the caretaker.

Caretaking is destructive to organizations in another way. It sends a hostile message to employees: "Unlike us (management), you're not capable of doing what others can do, so we'll have to do it for you." It is plantation paternalism at its worst. The two consequences of this demeaning system are (1) feelings of ungratefulness and entitlement; and (2) a need for revenge (people want to get back at those who demean them).

Despite these negative consequences, our organizations are set in their caretaking ways, which makes the transition to the caring for paradigm difficult. When you expect people to be responsible for themselves, when you tell people what they need to hear rather than what they want to hear, they frequently react defensively and become upset. When they become upset, management backs off, assuming that if employees are upset, management has done something wrong.

Just the opposite is true. That state of upsetness means you've hit a responsive chord. To help people embrace the new paradigm—and learn to work without the caretaking net—you need to stick to your guns during this period of discomfort. Remind yourself that what you're doing is designed to grow your people; it's not done because you dislike them or think they're mopes.

It isn't easy. I've had more than one person tell me about confronting an employee who wasn't doing his or her job effectively and about hating to see how unhappy those comments made that employee. In these instances, I often use my analogy from Chapter 1: "Just because you hated to see your toddler fall down when he walked, that doesn't mean you should stop him from walking."

To help you determine whether you (or people you work with) are stuck in the old caretaking paradigm, see if any or all of the following three caretaking traits apply to you. If they do, go on to the exercises (page 20) that will help you embrace the caring for paradigm.

CARETAKING TRAITS

- **Acceptance of irritating people.** "Every time he opens his mouth he irritates me," a manager says. But the manager never confronts this coworker with that fact; he simply suffers in silence. Failing to confront people with their negative qualities is a sure sign of caretaking.

- **Overlong, boring, and time-wasting meetings.** The goal of caretaking meetings is to make everyone happy and satisfied with the meeting's decisions. You spend many additional hours trying to achieve consensus while avoiding the critical issues— issues that will produce conflict.

- **Misplaced loyalty to long-term employees.** You give a pass to people who are no longer making contributions because of their length of service to the organization. Rather than confronting them with their lack of contribution or mistakes, you take care of them. In reality, you're doing nothing more than allowing them to live in a fool's paradise—if you leave or the company gets sold, they'll find themselves unprepared for the harsh reality of being unemployed.

SHIFTING MECHANISMS

Shifting from the old caretaking to the new caring for paradigm can be facilitated by the following three approaches:

- **Deal straightforwardly and immediately with sources of irritation.** Do a careful assessment of what the irritating employee does well and poorly. Explain why he or she irritates you and others and how that has a negative impact on his or her career and the organization. Suggest ways to change and correct that behavior, and make clear the consequences if the employee refuses to change. Nothing is less caring and more cruel than to withhold this valuable information from people who are performing below par.

- **Conduct meetings with the goal of 100 percent "online processing."** In other words, whenever a meeting is called, all key issues are discussed during the meeting. The goal is to resolve problems rather than to protect people. Executives are sometimes reluctant to bring up sensitive issues, such as why one area never delivers products or services effectively to another area. If this issue is discussed at all, it is done so in private, probably in a closed-door, one-on-one session. To eliminate this caretaking posture, discuss the issue with the group. Communicate that the meeting is not a personal attack but a way to resolve problems.

- **Tell people they're capable of changing the way they operate.** caring for managers believe and communicate that no matter who an employee is or how long he or she has worked at an organization, he or she can change and make a significant contribution. Even though the employee may not have made a contribution in years, that doesn't make him or her beyond redemption. The key here is to tell the employee what he or she must do to contribute and what the consequences are if he or she chooses not to. Avoiding this discussion may save the employee from emotional hurt in the short run; but it may also set him or her up for never working again.

PARADIGM 2: People's ability to change is not a function of capacity but of choice.

You *can* teach old dogs new tricks, but they have to want to learn them. The notion that veteran or any other types of employees can't change is nonsense. I don't subscribe to Peter Drucker's theory that people won't change much, so your only option is to alter their environment. I don't subscribe to it because I've seen all types of people—from CEOs to junior executives to assembly-line workers—make dramatic changes.

During the course of my work for one client, I dealt with some of their plant managers who had at least twenty-five years of experience with the company. For those twenty-five years, they were steeped in a culture where bad news was *verboten*. The culture dictated that plant managers should not be bothered with problems; that if there were problems, someone was doing something wrong and that person had better take care of it himself or herself.

When I started working with this organization, plant managers resisted any changes to this culture. The concept of being receptive to bad news, rewarding the person who brought it to their attention and then talking about how to solve problems was horrifying. The plant managers were stunned that they were being asked to make such monumental changes in their behavior.

Yet over time, almost all of them changed. After they had accepted the new paradigm, these plant managers said that they gradually began to feel like *different people*; that they no longer viewed themselves as cogs in some vast machine but understood how they fit into the larger organization and what and how they contributed to it. They all felt more committed to the company's goals than they ever had before.

Employees making a successful transition to a high risk culture need to learn why it's important to change from good soldiers to challenging employees. In the past, employees were paid to get work done in a prescribed manner and not to irritate the boss. In our new high risk culture, if employees fail to challenge bosses when things aren't right, they'll be fired.

However, many employees resist giving up their nets, as evidenced by the many failed total quality management (TQM) programs. Management doesn't understand that TQM requires employees to undergo this very transformation—from good soldiers to challenging employees. TQM also forever alters the employee's relationship with the company. These changes scare many employees and they react by resisting TQM, viewing it as the enemy.

The change resistance fostered by TQM is especially evident with middle managers. Much has been written about the "silo" mentality (an inability to think about work in a cross-functional manner; one's perspective is narrowly defined by one's job) of middle managers caught up in quality efforts. Middle managers have been accused of refusing to work cross-functionally (as TQM demands) but instead staying within their safe, comfortable functional areas. More than once, I've heard someone in top management say about a functional vice president, "He's never going to be able to work with guys from manufacturing, sales, or accounting." Why not? Is he brain damaged? We tend to depreciate our employees' ability to change. It is only when an organization places a cap on growth—where the culture has sanctions against new and different approaches—that middle managers cling to their silos.

The question isn't whether people can change, but whether they choose to change.

TEST YOUR CHANGE CAPACITY

You can test your attitude toward the change paradigm—as well as the attitudes of those you work with—by conducting the following exercise:

List ten employees you know relatively well. They can be a mix of subordinates, superiors, and coworkers. Next to each name, place a "c" or "nc"—the former letter for people you believe are capable of changing, the latter for those who you think are incapable of changing.

When you're done, count the number of nc's you listed. Even if you have only one nc, you're still stuck in the old paradigm. The new paradigm holds that everyone is capable, and the real question is whether they want to change.

PARADIGM 3: We need to change our attitudes toward change.

Most of us resist change until it's irresistible. We've been raised in a culture that considers change to be bad and the status quo to be good. However, people are starting to realize that things can't remain the same—if the Japanese and the global economy have taught us nothing, they have taught us that. So we give lip service to change. I've had clients tell me, "Oh, we like change. We just put in a fax machine." But they'll still try to build consensus with customers as they've done for years rather than taking the riskier but far more productive approach of challenging them.

The new paradigm is not diametrically opposed to the old one. It doesn't advocate blindly accepting every change that comes down the road. Instead, it requires analysis of what's new and different and making informed decisions so that the right changes can be made. The new paradigm means we must become perpetual evaluators, because those are the people who can make informed decisions. Building self-esteem is also part of this construct. If you don't feel good about yourself, you'll become rigid and resistant to change. With high self-esteem, however, you possess the necessary confidence to try something new and different. You'll realize that you don't need your safety net.

None of this is easy. We're trying to unlearn 40,000 years of fight-or-flight response to change. When a predator crossed our path, adrenaline poured through our system and we reacted instantly. We aren't biochemically built to take a step back, scratch our chins, and evaluate. But if we learn to step back and evaluate, we can override our long-standing historical response to stress and change.

CHANGE PARADIGM EXERCISE

Consider the following four hypothetical situations:

- Your company asks you to relocate.

- Your organization is taken over by a foreign company.

- You're asked to change the traditional way you do your job because a new program is being introduced (like TQM).

- Your boss of many years retires and is replaced by a new boss with a very different type of management style.

Is your reaction to these situations along the lines of

A. I (or we) can't do it; I quit; You're crazy.

or

B. I have to investigate the possibility; it might be worth trying.

Reaction A is indicative of the old paradigm, Reaction B of the new one.

PARADIGM 4: *We must redefine what constitutes acceptable work, moving from adequacy to peak performance.*

We've taught people to do things to get them done. In the low-change, slow-pace world of the 1950s, such a paradigm was fine. But we continue to hold employees to this undemanding standard, asking that they just finish what they started in a reasonable time frame. Management often believes that to demand anything beyond that from its workers would be demanding too much.

If that is true, how do you explain the productivity gains American workers have made in recent years? Mercedes announced that it was building a plant in North Carolina because it found that whereas it takes a German worker an average of thirty hours to build a car, it takes an American worker twenty-four hours. This is only one example of the tremendous productivity gains Americans have made, and they've come primarily because more has been demanded from people and they've responded positively.

But for the most part, we've made mediocrity our standard. Despite all the corporate slogans about superior performance, organizations accept mere competency. The reasoning goes that superior is a nice ideal, but it's not reality; that most employees aren't capable of the effort superior requires; that employees who put forth that effort will burn out.

Organizations like IBM and GM—companies that were highly profitable in the past—are especially vulnerable to this mentality. As the money rolls in, management is lulled into believing that it shouldn't ask too much of its people. If it does, the unions might protest; the workers' morale might go down. Why risk such demands when they're making money hand over fist? Because they won't be for long. It's no coincidence that the organizations that suffered the most in the recent recession were formerly the most profitable. As George Romney of the now-defunct American Motors once said, "Nothing is more dangerous than entrenched profitability."

One of the premises of the new paradigm is: If you're going to demand a lot of employees, they have to like their jobs. Our organizations are filled with people who show far more enthusiasm for projects they work on in their basements than projects they work on in their offices. The old paradigm dictated that you didn't have to like what you did as long as you were able to do it and it paid the bills. So we ended up with many employees who either did just enough to get by or, driven by the old Protestant work ethic, literally slaved away at a job they hated and eventually burned out. When people do what they like, however, they are willing to work harder, longer, and better.

The question, of course, is how to move all those people from jobs they dislike to ones they like. With the old paradigm, the answer would be impossible: a caretaking approach of massive retraining and reeducation. But we over complicate the job-learning process. Most jobs don't require rocket science. Many organizations are burdened by the misconception, perhaps fostered by educators, that to do a job properly, you need formal education. Although this education might add to one's knowledge base, it rarely adds the skills necessary to do a job.

Under the new paradigm, the answer is apprenticeships and support and demand for personal and professional growth. One of my clients, in breaking with its 120-year-old tradition of caretaking, rewrote its employee manual. Instead of the usual emphasis on all the wonderful things the company gives to its employees, a clear and unmistakable caveat was issued: "You are responsible for your personal and professional growth." Demanding and facilitating growth through information and accountability increases commitment and empowers achievement.

In the new paradigm, people need to be as passionate about their jobs as they are about a beloved hobby. It is the only way that they can meet an organization's demand for peak performance and the culture's demand for continued growth and marketability. Aggregate numbers, average group performance and the anomaly of individual overextension have no place in a high risk, globally driven economy. The goal of peak performance from every employee must be met while eliminating mediocrity, minimal compliance, and marginal commitment. If nonpeak performance remains the standard, chronic unemployment will persist.

A TEST FOR PEAK CAPACITY

The following is a simple but effective test to determine the paradigm an employee embraces:

> *When you (or your employee) receive an assignment, is your first question*
> *A. How much can I get done by the end of the day?*
> > *or*
> *B. When does this need to be done?*
>
> *Question A indicates a clock orientation, representative of adequacy. Question B indicates a project orientation, representative of peak performance.*
>
> *A supplementary test question would be to ask yourself (or your employee), "Are you doing a given task to make your boss happy or because it is the best way to turn out quality work?"*

There are many formerly happy bosses out there who have been bankrupted by adequate performance. If a boss doesn't permit anything but mediocrity, challenge him or her. If that doesn't work, quit. Above all else, don't be a victim.

PARADIGM 5: Who we are personally is inextricably connected to who we are professionally; the goal is to lead blended, not balanced, lives.

Though the days of sweat shops and chain gangs are gone, we still treat work as the worst kind of torture and our personal life as a refuge from work. The old balanced-life paradigm emphasizes separating our time at home from our time on the job. However, the result is an impossible balancing act. Home and work are two completely separate entities pulling us in opposite directions and off balance. Now that the net is gone, we need to redistribute the load.

The new paradigm, on the other hand, maintains that how you operate personally affects the way you operate professionally (and vice versa). If you have trouble with personal relationships, you'll have trouble with professional ones. If you try and control every aspect of your teenagers' lives and treat them like total incompetents, you'll treat your employees the same way.

For example, there is a middle manager whose personal life is the envy of all who know him. He and his wife seem to be the perfect couple. They're both attractive and in terrific shape; they have a beautiful house, wonderful friends, and a couple of terrific kids. Anyone who has observed this couple would say they get along better than most people; that they never get into arguments and no one has ever seen the other utter a cross word. At work, however, this middle manager is experiencing problems. His superior and colleagues note that he hasn't had any professional growth in the past five years; that he has plateaued; that he is unable to initiate contact with others, failing to ask necessary questions of customers and coworkers.

At first glance, it would seem that this middle manager has a perfect personal life and an imperfect professional one. At least that is the conclusion a casual observer would draw. But if we could look behind closed doors, we would find that this man's personal life has serious problems. Specifically, he hasn't had sex with his wife for seven years; he never talks with his wife about anything beyond mundane, superficial matters; he hasn't made a new friend in years, and his relationships with old friends have become nothing more than casual social interactions. Personally and professionally, our middle manager is living in an emotional desert—his relationship with his wife and friends is reflected in his relationship with coworkers and customers.

I realize this is a complex and controversial subject, and I'll be dealing with it in much more detail in later chapters. For now, I want to clear up some common misconceptions that crop up whenever I introduce this paradigm.

First, the personal/professional mix doesn't translate into institutionalized workaholism. Though you'll have to work harder in the future, you won't lose your private life. But you'll lead a much more structured life. Without structure, you'll be overwhelmed. You won't be able to take advantage of the numerous opportunities and rewards that come your way if either your personal or professional lives are chaotic.

Second, there's the myth of "we've been doing fine without it (personal/professional integration)." I've been asked why this blending is necessary since people have separated their work and personal existences for years without negative consequences. What about consequences such as a 68 percent job dissatisfaction rate; or massive codependency; or the pervasive drug problem? A clear connection exists between unintegrated lives and these dysfunctional areas.

Third, don't assume that because this paradigm makes you uncomfortable, there's something wrong with it. So many of us view our personal lives as necessary escapes from work, from the pressure-filled, daily grind. Without that escape, you may be thinking, I'll go nuts! But why do you need an escape? What if work were as good as your personal life? In a high risk culture, you'd better like your work or you won't be doing it for long.

BLENDING YOUR LIFE

If you're wondering whether you're leading a blended or balanced life, the following question, exercise, and action plan will help you arrive at an answer:

1. QUESTION: How often do you say, "I should have done this" or "I ought to do that"? If you regularly make these statements, you're striving for an impossible balance. You're staying late at

work but saying you ought to be home; you're going on vacation but you tell your spouse you should be at an industry conference.

2. EXERCISE: Write down three key roles in your life (choose from parent, spouse, employee, manager, friend, and so on). Next to each role, list your assets and liabilities in performing that role. Then ask the following:

- Do people recognize what your assets are?

- Do other people demand that you perform tasks that you've classified as liabilities?

- Are you trying to do things in each role that encompass both your assets and liabilities—being all things to all people?

3. ACTION PLAN: Talk to people and be up front about what your liabilities are; ask other people to assist you in finding ways to accomplish tasks that you don't do well. For instance, you might say to a colleague, "I'm lousy at this detail work; maybe we can structure the job so that this work gets done without me screwing it up." Or, you might explain to your family that you hate baseball, and rather than attending every one of your son's little league games, mom and sister (who enjoy baseball) will attend the majority of them. The point is to find alternative approaches to meet other people's needs (blended) rather than forcing yourself to try and meet all of them (balanced).

PARADIGM 6: *We must create value-driven personal and professional lives.*

Think for a minute about how most organizations have addressed the coalescence of values among employees, what I call "value confluence." The thinking under the old paradigm goes, "We don't have the right to impose our values on others." As a result, the organization's values are never defined and stipulated. Executive A has one set of values, and Executive B has a completely different set. "We respect other people's values," is the way management defends this value mix. What they really mean is, "We have no idea how to deal with these different values so we'll just ignore the issue."

Without shared, core values, everyone does his or her own thing. Lacking a guidance system, the values they adhere to may have no connection with organizational values. Without value confluence, people run off in different directions. Teamwork becomes impossible in all but the most superficial sense of the term. No connection exists between organizational values and how employees perform their jobs.

For instance, a top manager espouses all the right values, eloquently communicating the importance of relationship building within the organization. But this manager also has an assistant who sits outside his office like a dragon at the gates. He is intolerant and intolerable; everyone dreads dealing with him. As a result, the manager's talk about building relationships is undermined by the relationship-destroying assistant.

Another corporation is run by a CEO whose values include responsiveness and a sense of urgency in building relationships. The CEO applies this belief in his relationships with friends and family and also with the company's customers. But this core value starts and stops with the CEO. A seemingly minor but very significant illustration of value dissonance is evidenced by the way the receptionist answers the phone. When a customer calls asking for an executive, the dialogue is as follows:

> **Receptionist:** *I don't know if he's here, he doesn't tell me when he leaves.*

> **Customer:** *Will he be in this afternoon?*

> **Receptionist:** *How do I know?*

> **Customer:** *Well, does he usually come in during the afternoon?*

> **Receptionist:** *Sometimes I see him, sometimes I don't.*

I asked the head of the company how he could tolerate this type of behavior. He replied that the receptionist came from a disadvantaged background where common courtesy wasn't particularly important. Besides, he added, "she's been answering the phone this way for ten years and we don't expect her to change now. It's just the way she is."

The way she is violates the organization's core values. People who do so must be confronted, and if they can't share those values, they have no place in the organization. As painful a process as this is, it's absolutely necessary. In a high risk culture, value dissonance is lethal.

Value confluence can only be achieved through the combination of statement and action. It's not enough to say that based on our core values, no one is allowed to verbally abuse the clerical staff. This must be backed up with reinforcing behaviors. Even if the company's best salesperson harasses her secretary, top management must make it clear to her that her actions won't be tolerated, and if she persists, she will be fired.

In the new paradigm, value confluence exists personally and professionally. At home, clearly defined and adhered-to values catalyze individual and family growth and development. At work, they are the foundation for all business decisions, from choosing suppliers to targeting customers. Recruiting, marketing, promotion, vendor relationships—all emerge from a value base. Successful organizations place value confluence in every area at the top of their lists, far above taking the most expedient actions.

The following questions will give you a sense if you and your organization are value confluent or value dissonant.

TEST YOUR ORGANIZATION'S VALUE CONFLUENCE

QUESTIONS

1. Does your organization face the same problem or conflict month after month, year after year?
2. Is there a person (or people) in your company who others postpone dealing with because he or she is so abrasive, inarticulate, indecisive, etc., or only do so as a last resort?
3. Does your company buy goods or services from a supplier it doesn't particularly like only because it's the lowest-cost supplier?
4. Does your organization generally hire people with the right experience over people who may lack the requisite education or training but who "feel" right to the interviewer?
5. When major internal problems occur, do people react with hostility (as opposed to rational discussion)?

ANSWERS

1. Recurrent problems or conflicts are indicative of value dissonance. On the other hand, a value-confluent organization may
   have problems, but those problems are constantly changing.
2. This is a sure sign of value dissonance in a high risk culture—
   not only are people avoiding conflict, they're avoiding contact.
3. What a company really is saying in this instance is, "We can be
   had if the price is right."
4. This is a common hiring debate: to take the person who feels
   right versus the one whose credentials look right. Relying primarily on objective criteria often means ignoring values. I've
   found it's far more effective to hire someone who resonates to
   the company's core values; you can teach skills and build experience much easier than you can create values.
5. Any organization where threats and ultimatums are common is
   suffering from value dissonance. When people don't believe
   management shares their values, they resort to hostility to solve
   problems. In value-confluent companies, negotiation takes the
   place of threats.

A NEW WAY TO VIEW THE WORLD

The six paradigms discussed in this chapter aren't discrete rules for
the future. Each is connected to the other. Though we've suggested
some of the connections, the linkages will become much clearer in
following chapters. For now, you should understand that paradigms
form new parameters for living and working in a changing culture.
The old paradigms, which I've referred to, provided ground rules for
living and working in a static culture.

Because our culture is changing so quickly, we must learn to
accept and embrace the new paradigms. Countless examples illustrate those cultural changes. In the 1980s, the model of a business
leader was a one-minute manager who was stone faced and close
mouthed about nonbusiness matters; now we have business management teams going on retreats to get in touch with their feelings. Here
is a shocking set of statistics. In the not-too-distant past, American
business was consistently ranked among the biggest and best in every

industry. In a 1992 report, Morgan Stanley points out that seven of ten of the biggest automobile companies are non-American; ten of the ten largest banks are non-American; eight of the ten largest utilities are non-American. Finally, a study shows that by the year 2000, 85 percent of the workforce will be working for companies with fewer than 200 employees—what happened to big business?

The new paradigms should help ground you internally so you're not dazed and confused by the lightning pace of change. They provide order and structure in a world that suddenly seems to lack either of those organizing principles. That order and structure is crucial as you function in a high risk culture without a net.

C H A P T E R
THE IMPACT OF INFORMATION ON COMPETITIVE ADVANTAGE

The catalyst for the creation of the six paradigms described in Chapter 2 is *information*. The information revolution has transformed our world, and the odds are that your gut has already sensed that transformation, even if your conscious mind hasn't. You've sensed that things have changed; that the old behaviors at work were no longer being rewarded. People often are scared by what their gut tells them. People feel tense, off balance. They don't want to admit to themselves that they're working without a net.

All the old rules have disappeared. The new rules of the business world are the paradigms discussed in Chapter 2. In this chapter, I'd like to explain how information changed the rules and shaped these paradigms, especially as they apply to the world of business. Then I'll discuss what you can do to take advantage of the new rules.

We saw the power of information technology to effect change in the late 1960s, as the Vietnam War was broadcast into our homes. Never before had we experienced continuous, traumatic events in our living rooms. Never before had we witnessed these events as they were unfolding. The immediacy of that information forced us to make decisions and judgments about what we were viewing; we no longer had the cushion of time, reading about these events three weeks after the fact. Seeing the dead bodies and weeping families forced us not only to make decisions about the war, but to acknowledge our vulnerability.

The new and improved transmission of information shaped our high risk culture in other ways. It helped break down the world's ideological polarization, showing people that other options existed besides the rigid ideologies they had known all their lives. But as the ideological polarization melted, the linked economic fate of nations was forged. During the cold war, it didn't seem to matter what the Communists did (economically) because they were frozen out of our capitalist system. Now, what happens in Russia and other former communist bloc countries has a tremendous impact on Americans and American corporations.

Information also has the power to change expectations. As more information enters people's lives, the more their expectations are raised and changed.

More than any other factor, information has ripped away our safety nets, making it impossible to ignore changes in the world around us. The technologies of fax machines, overnight delivery, and electronic mail (e-mail) have virtually altered time and space. National boundaries vanish; virtual corporations form and dissipate like passing clouds. Even Wall Street is no longer on Wall Street:

> Wall Street today has transformed itself into a virtually seamless network of computer-linked brokers, dealers and exchanges around the globe. . . . The trades take place in an electronic neverland that can be entered from anywhere in the world. Billion-dollar transactions involving derivatives or other securities that once took hours or days to handle are now routinely completed in seconds—with all the potential risk or reward that comes with instant gains and losses.[1]

We receive information more quickly and must also respond to that information quickly. Because of fax machines and modems, "I'll get you that report next week" has become, "I'll get you that report

---

[1] John Greenwald, "The Secret Money Machine," *Time*, April 11, 1994, p. 33.

this afternoon." You might also be working as closely with colleagues on another continent as with those down the hall. The way we think of "my company" is shifting away from the people we work with at the office to something less solid, more amorphous.

EXPECT NEW EXPECTATIONS

Information also has the power to change expectations. As more information enters people's lives, the more their expectations are raised and changed.

We are perfectly content one day, but the next day we attend a conference that makes us discontent with our jobs, our careers, our lives. We see new possibilities, and the status quo no longer fulfills our needs. It may not take a day; it can happen in the span of a television program or the time it takes to read an article. When expectations change rapidly, nothing is predictable.

Unpredictability, one element of a high risk culture, is evident in the following example.

A North American nickel mining company, the largest such mining operation in the world, had to fire 5,000 people in the wake of the Soviet Union's collapse. Both the collapse and its impact on this mining company would have been difficult to predict. The nickel mining operation suffered because immediately after the collapse, most of the barbed wire in the Soviet Union and its satellite countries was melted down. The price of nickel was driven down by this action because nickel is a major component of barbed wire. The reduced price forced the mine to terminate a significant percentage of its workforce.

Information's impact on business manifests itself in countless less dramatic but no less significant ways. For example, I've heard employees complain, "This is the third time this month the boss has changed his mind about how we do *x* in this department. He obviously doesn't know what he's doing." Employees are nervous—and annoyed at the rework involved—when a boss keeps changing directions. However, those changes may be essential and based on new information the boss has received. Instead of being an incompetent jerk, the boss may be responding quickly and appropriately in a dynamic situation.

Information's impact on business is not limited to employee

anxiety over a fickle boss. In fact, information's three critical impacts are

- Increased competition

- Decreased profits and margins

- Heightened emphasis on human resources as the key to gaining a competitive edge

IMPACT ONE:
INCREASED COMPETITION

Information produces highly educated consumers. They see a television news special about a car's dangerous gas tank and they refuse to buy that car; they read an article about an alternative medical treatment for a stubborn ailment, and they'll demand that their doctors at least consider the new treatment. The goods and services they settled for yesterday won't suffice today. Organizations that refuse to respond to rising consumer expectations and demands for the new and the better will lose out to competitors who do respond. Constantly shifting and rising consumer demands force organizations into permanent growth and change modes—they are in a battle with competitors to respond more quickly to changing demands.

Competition is also heating up because few secrets stay secret for long in an information-intensive culture. The more companies know about what makes a market tick, the easier it is for them to enter that market. For years, insurance sales were the sole domain of insurance companies. But as banks learned they could make more money selling insurance policies than mortgages, they entered this new and more profitable market. Information also fueled a tobacco company's entrance into the food marketing arena and a clothing manufacturer's decision to manufacture steel. When an organization attends a conference on global marketing and hears about opportunities in third world countries, it starts the transition from national to international company.

Some organizations assume a defensive posture in the face of this increased competition. Embracing old paradigms, they view competition as a life-or-death athletic contest—only one gladiator can survive. They compete by attacking—charging that a competitor's products harm the environment, for instance. A sense of desperate struggle pervades their competitive efforts. They are terrified of competing in our culture because they believe resources are scarce—they're convinced that their market is shrinking.

Other organizations view increased competition as an opportunity to define and enhance their unique strengths. Embracing the new paradigms, they believe that there can be many winners in any given marketplace, as long as companies distinguish themselves from others. They believe in infinite resources—information-driven competition is creating opportunities that never existed before.

Which view of competition does your organization hold? To take advantage of the latter perspective, organizations should pose the following questions:

1. *What do we do that's different from others in our industry; why should customers deal with us rather than competitors?*

2. *If there is no significant difference between us and competitors, what might create a difference in consumers' minds? If this issue has never been addressed, is it because we fall back on the argument that people buy from us because we do what we do very well? Do other companies in our industry do what they do very well?*

3. *How might we change the way we operate to do things both differently and well? Is our "difference" relationship driven (as opposed to product or service driven)?*

IMPACT TWO: DECREASED PROFITS AND MARGINS

"Why can't we make the same profits we did a few years ago? After all, we still come up with great products and services, our marketing efforts are terrific, we're doing the same things that worked before. What's wrong?"

The one-word answer to that last, commonly asked question is *replicability*. Because so much information is available to so many competitors so quickly, replicating a successful product or service is relatively easy. The days of cornering a market are over. In the past, corporations would milk a great product for years, confident that it would take a long time for competitors to catch up. With today's information technology, nothing remains secret or unique for very long. Build a better mousetrap and the world may still beat a path to your door, but they won't stay for long.

Of course, this notion drives engineers and research and development (R&D)-driven organizations crazy. Because the shelf life of innovation has been truncated each year, the premise that innovation breeds success has been undermined. Although great R&D is still necessary, it now only gets you to the starting line; it doesn't ensure a winning race.

Furthermore, being the marketer of a premium or high-quality product no longer guarantees success. Whether it is IBM with computers or (ironically) Xerox with copiers, a terrific product can and will be replicated. Brand loyalty won't last in the face of an equal-quality knockoff at a lower price. For years, Kodak ruled the roost as a marketer of premium film. But as information reached consumers telling them that generic film at a lower price wasn't much different from Kodak, many of Kodak's formerly loyal customers switched to generic brands of film.

Similarly, margins shrink when companies come into the marketplace with knockoffs priced below the original to steal away customers. Typically, the originator of the product counters with its own price reductions, creating a price war that reduces margins.

The artificial competitive edge patents give companies is also beginning to become a thing of the past. Many organizations are finding that much of what they would like to patent is in the public domain, and what they can patent is only some small piece of the total product design. Any organization that focuses the bulk of its effort on R&D is fooling itself if it thinks such a focus will yield a big competitive edge.

I recently had a conversation on a plane with my seat partner, a vice president for a multinational corporation, that illustrates this point. When I asked him what his job was, he told me that he "sold his company's R&D to the competition." I asked him to run that one by me again. He explained that his company realized that because of the accessibility of information about its products, competitors were going to discover what they needed to know one way or another. His company decided on the sensible approach of funding its own R&D by selling the fruit of that labor to others in the industry.

Given the many factors responsible for declining profits and margins, how should an organization respond? Traditionally, organizations have responded to falling profits by encouraging their people to work longer and harder, the logic being that such increased labor results in productivity gains or more sales. Consider the following question: Are you working harder and longer (either as an individual or an organization) than you ever did before but making the same or less money? Most people answer that question affirmatively. The problem is that all that hard work reaches a point of diminishing returns or burns out people. The following two questions will lead you to an alternative approach:

1. *Is everyone in your organization pulling 100 percent of his or her weight, or are some people carrying others? Most organizations have at least a few martyrs—overachieving individuals who are highly productive, compensating for those who are dead weight.*

2. *Is everyone in your organization doing highly profitable work at his or her skill level? The odds are that many highly skilled managers are spending their time on projects that yield little or no profit; they're doing low- or no-profit work that they never should have been doing in the first place.*

EXERCISE: SKILLS, PROFITS TIME RELATIONSHIP

Choose three key people in your organization and write down their names. Next to each name, list the person's major skill (or skills) that translates into profit for the organization. Estimate the percentage of time each person devotes to practicing that skill on the job (for instance, John spends 50 percent of his time exercising his selling skill and the other 50 percent of the time on paperwork). Anything less than 90 percent is unacceptable (in the new paradigm of peak performance).

IMPACT THREE: PEOPLE ARE THE COMPETITIVE EDGE

Unlike products or services, the distinctive, idiosyncratic nature of relationships is very difficult to replicate. Information has ensured replicability of every competitive advantage except the relationship between a seller and a buyer. The same sweater is available at roughly the same price at five different retailers. But the retailer that gets the most business (and most repeat business) is the one that focuses on relationships; their salespeople can provide customers with valuable advice not only about the sweater, but whether it goes with the other clothes they're considering purchasing. Another example is the vendor who prints and binds your product catalog. There are thousands of other companies that can do the same job and would quote a lower cost. But you stay with the vendor that works smoothly with your marketing staff and can be trusted to deliver your catalogs to the mailing department on time.

Though I'll go into detail later in this book about the relationship-building skills organizations require in a high risk culture, I should clarify what relationship-building *isn't*. It isn't the *greeter* in a big store slapping customers on their backs and thanking them for shopping there. It isn't taking purchasing managers out to dinner and calling them regularly. That's schmoozing, not relationship-building. That's the old caretaking paradigm, not the new caring for model. Challenge, confrontation, and conflict management are the real skills of relationship-building. Telling customers what they need to know ("The cheaper paper won't allow the color printing quality you want") rather than what they want to hear ("Sure, we can print your catalog on lower-priced paper") is essential.

People will pay virtually any price for information they need. A recent insurance industry survey revealed that 95 percent of the most successful agencies use outside consultants, and 98 percent were totally satisfied with those consultants. The reason they're satisfied is that consultants tell them what they need to know, something their own people won't do.

Do you tell people what they need to know? Does your organization encourage such an approach? Consider the following two companies and see if you can tell which one answered yes to these questions.

COMPANY A

- Their culture's number-one priority is helping people be happy and comfortable in their work.

- They lavish praise on and reassure their employees, rarely if ever confronting them.

- They emphasize short-term results and never examine the process by which the results were achieved.

COMPANY B

- They are less concerned if their employees are comfortable and happy and more concerned that they are growing.

- They regularly assess their employees' strengths and weaknesses and require them to address areas of improvement.

- They create action plans for employees designed to improve a specific skill, attitude, or behavior.

The employees of Company B are a competitive asset. The company's encouragement of honest and open relationships permeates the culture and leads to productive relationships inside and outside the organization.

BUT WHAT ABOUT PRICE?

If information has robbed organizations of traditional differentiating tools, doesn't price become more important than ever before as the last and best way to differentiate? Isn't it as important or even more important than relationship-building?

These questions lead us to a choice facing every organization: whether to be a transactional or relationship driven business. Transactional businesses, like Wal-Mart, attract customers who only care about one thing: buying the cheapest product. In every market, there are customers who fit this description, and the information revolution has certainly made the lowest price more attractive to them. No doubt, Wal-Mart makes a great deal of money.

But any organization that chooses a transaction-driven business should understand that they're going to exhaust themselves beating the bushes to scare up that migratory bird, the price-buying customer. Organizations will find themselves engaged in a frantic seasonal hunt for people who want to buy cheap. Their cost of acquiring that customer will be higher than relationship-driven businesses, because they'll need big ad budgets to reach them with their low-price message. Just as problematic, these organizations will enjoy no customer loyalty—cease to be the lowest-cost provider and customers will flee. Just as a gunfighter eventually meets someone who is a little faster on the draw, transaction-driven companies always encounter someone willing to sell a little cheaper.

Put yourself in the customer's shoes. Perhaps you can find a vendor who will produce your product catalogs at a lower cost. But if the vendor misses your delivery date, or if the catalogs contain errors, you will lose sales. Or perhaps your marketing and creative people find the low-cost vendor a pain to work with; a great deal more staff time must be spent in follow-up to see to it that the job is done properly. The lower cost per unit may not be a bargain.

Retailers who sell on price alone get caught in this trap, which is why they voice the following refrain: "I dread every January." They dread it because they wonder where the next batch of low-price customers is going to come from. A relationship-driven business doesn't have that fear; they know their customers will return for the one thing no competitor can replicate: the unique relationship between seller and buyer.

Most bargain-hunting customers are not long-term customers. When these customers' expectations and circumstances rise, they no longer search desperately for the best deal. When they didn't have much money, they didn't care about who sold them a product or service. Now that they have more money, they are looking for a specific value-added interface with the seller. For instance, the price-driven customer may buy stock through a discount brokerage because he feels he can't afford to do otherwise. But as he has more money to invest and learns that there is more to be gained from the seller than just a good price, he will opt for a broker who will do more than sell. The broker must challenge the customer by saying, "Stock A is bad for your portfolio because. . ." or "You complain about your low returns, but are you willing to increase your risk and change your portfolio mix to increase the returns?" The movement from price buying to relationship-building is a one-way street; once customers realize the advantages of the latter, they never go back to the former.

BEING OPEN TO INFORMATION

Successful people are information hounds. They are hungry for every scrap of information that comes their way. They are receptive to everything, even if the source is untraditional and the facts are controversial.

This attitude toward information enables individuals and organizations to increase their options; they are more likely to come upon a crucial idea or fact than someone with a closed mind. Being aware of and taking advantage of information's impact on business depends on this receptivity. An organization that closes itself off to new trends, concepts, studies, and strategies will wonder why its profits and margins are declining each year even though it's still producing good products and services; it will also opt for a transactional rather than a relationship-driven business.

Being open to information means taking in a tremendous diversity of facts. Though most people only use a small fraction of what they take in, they never know until they scan everything what particular idea will prove valuable.

When it comes to untraditional or alternative ideas, organizations and managers may want to remember how quickly the unusual becomes the routine. One of the hottest speakers on the business lecture circuit is Depak Chopra, the Harvard University professor who combines Eastern and Western concepts. He talks about business as an organism and uses other unusual analogies. Not so long ago, people thought Chopra and this sort of talk were nutty.

Sometimes people dismiss information because they can't easily make the connection between disparate sources of knowledge. When either positive or negative change occurs in an organization, people experience feelings of loss. For profitable organizational growth to occur, people need to understand and deal with those feelings. The grieving process, which I will discuss in Chapter 8, facilitates this understanding. In many instances, however, people don't make the connection between a change that's occurred at work and the concept of loss. They don't immediately grasp the relationship between rapid growth (change) and the grieving process (the need to grieve a loss).

Some organizations are bewildered by the amount of information that flows to them, and they need a sorting mechanism to deal with that information effectively. As we'll see, a sorting mechanism is critical to the success of any information-driven company moving through the information cycle.

C H A P T E R
DECISION MAKING AND THE INFORMATION CYCLE

Given the information-intensive culture just described, two skills are essential for working without a net: decision-making and relationship-building. These skills are crucial for implementing the six paradigm shifts both personally and professionally. I'll focus on decision-making here and relationship-building in the next chapter. To understand why decision-making skills are so crucial, let's examine the information cycle.

The four elements of that cycle—information, choices, decisions, and change—are inextricably linked. As you can see from looking at the progression of the cycle, information generates choices that never existed before; the choices, in turn, call for decisions to be made; when decisions are made, change naturally occurs; and when change takes place, new information is generated, and the cycle starts all over again.

Let's examine the movement from one element of the cycle to the next in greater depth.

FROM INFORMATION TO CHOICES

This cycle begins with information-catalyzing choices. When we read about the effectiveness of an alternative channel of distribution

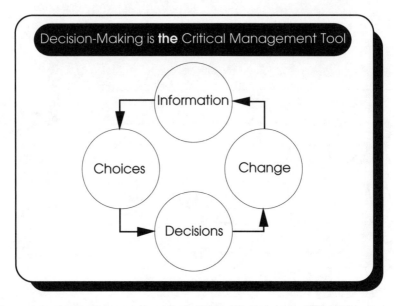

in a trade magazine, we suddenly have a choice we had never considered before. When we learn of a study that suggests that our technology is obsolete, we are presented with another choice. The more information we receive, the more choices we have.

In the past, information was limited, as were choices. Previous generations could go for a relatively long time without being confronted by alternatives to their traditional way of doing things. Today, we can't get up in the morning without facing a staggering number of options. If you live in or near a large city, just getting to work is an exercise in strategic and tactical planning. The first thing you do when you get up in the morning is listen to the traffic report and start strategizing. Compare this to your grandfather, who probably took the same route (and the same streetcar) all his working life.

Job choices have similarly multiplied. Years ago, people joined the family business, chose the profession of a parent, or worked for the community's major employer. Today, middle-class children have virtually unlimited choices. Not only does information make them acutely aware of these choices, but it can overwhelm them. It's overwhelming because most young people don't possess a sorting mechanism—a method for dealing with all the choices presented to them. Unlike previous generations, young adults have relatively little occupational experience to draw on to sort choices. Besides a few meaningless summer jobs, they have never served an apprenticeship or contributed to the family by working. The great irony is that children from affluent families are given more choices than anyone else, but they are also less prepared than anyone to handle those choices.

As a result, they're overwhelmed, and they often respond to that feeling by voluntarily relinquishing their power of choice. This is why cults attract so many middle-class kids. Information-intensive cultures are breeding grounds for cults. The cults tell people, there's only one choice to make, and that's us; give us your money and we'll take care of you and tell you what to believe and what to do. The rise of fundamentalism, too, parallels the rise of our information-intensive culture. Fundamentalists take away the agony of choice with their absolute, inflexible system of belief.

Some companies attract people for the same reasons. Their philosophy, "Don't think about it, just do it," appeals to those overwhelmed by choices. But when this type of organization must change to survive, its change-resistant employees freak out. The prospect of a slew of new choices scares them to death.

In recent years, we've seen many organizations that have responded to information and its concomitant choices with rigidity instead of flexibility. General Motors received data that indicated that Japanese car companies were doing a superior job of meeting consumer demand. Instead of confronting the choices mandated by that information—changing the way they ran their factories, for instance—they told their people: "Don't worry, keep doing what you're doing, don't panic."

FROM CHOICES TO DECISIONS

Organizations and individuals must respond to information by making choices. Yet time after time, they freeze, and nothing is more destructive to the health of the individual or the business. Research indicates a strong connection between indecision and illness. The theory behind this is that all the energy created by the body to handle the decision isn't released; instead, the energy implodes and causes disease. In the same way, organizations that refuse to decide begin deteriorating. A consumer electronics company learns that a competitor's new compact disc player contains a feature that supposedly creates a richer sound, and the product is selling like hotcakes. Based on this information, the company has two choices: to produce their own new CD player with the same type of feature; or to communicate to the marketplace that the company's current CD player produces sound that is as rich as the competitor's.

Instead of making a choice, they dither—they launch a study because they feel that they need more information before they decide. In the meantime, consumers are coming into stores and asking if the company's product has the competitor's feature. The salesperson says no. Then they ask if the current product is as good as the one with the feature. The salesperson, who hasn't heard from the company's sales reps on this subject, can only shrug. Naturally, consumers flock to the competing product.

REGRET-FREE DECISIONS

So we must learn to make decisions. But we must also learn to make them quickly and without regret. When one person fails to make a decision quickly, the window of opportunity closes; a more decisive person does what he or she should have done. Similarly, many organizations have been slow to enter a new market and then watched with dismay as a competitor took it by storm.

Delaying a decision has other negative consequences. Delay a decision by as little as one day and the decision radically changes. When you delay, you never have the same decision to make again because in an information-intensive culture, the facts are different the next day or the next week. But organizations often delude themselves and determine that they'll take it slow and wait three months before determining what to do. They incorrectly assume that in three months, nothing much will change.

Before all of you become one-second decision makers, let me emphasize the difference between fast and impulsive decision-making. Fast decision-making is not synonymous with snap, fact-deficient decisions. The snap-decision mindset means, don't bother me with assets and liabilities, let's do it because the other guys are. It is a nonevaluative approach. When companies rush out new products only because their competitors have, that is impulsive decision-making. Fast decision-making requires people to be trained like high-speed computers: to weigh assets and liabilities, consider the balance, and then make a decision. It also demands short time frames:

Someone determines up front that if the decision isn't made in a week, the opportunity will have been lost.

Regret-free decisions, the other critical attribute, means maintaining a decision-making mode even though a certain percentage of decisions will be viewed as mistakes. Our tendency to second guess decisions and quickly reverse them manifests itself throughout corporate America. Memos are issued and rescinded with regularity. Management takes a bold step forward followed by a timid step backward. The CEO makes a pronouncement that the organization is completely committed to a project and then backs away from the commitment when costs rise higher than expected. Indecisiveness destroys credibility. Employees' attitudes become, "This too shall pass." They're certain that they can wait out a given manager or fad; that after a period of time, it will be gone—middle managers call this the *idea du jour* syndrome. When this attitude is present, employees are cynical and see no reason to adapt to change.

We need to accept that mistakes are part of the decision-making process. But we shouldn't assume that people are inherently poor decision-makers. The problem does not always lie in the evaluation of data, but in the rapidly changing data that were not available at the time of the decision. Despite the old saw that people should gather *all the data* before making a decision, we will never have all the data we need in this culture. Data are constantly being produced that was not available at the time of the decision. *All the data* is like the concept of infinity—you can only approach it but never get there.

Regret-free decision-making is antithetical to risk-free decision-making. Risk can no longer be eliminated. In the past, you could live with the illusion of safety longer because information didn't arrive as fast. Because the information on which we base our decisions can change overnight, there are no sure things. You may enter into an agreement to import goods from the nation of New Utopia, only to have the U.S. State Department slap trade sanctions on New Utopia the next day. You may decide to design your product around a promising new technology, only to find that an even better technology has been developed before your new product is even ready to ship to retailers. In either case, the original decisions were not bad, they simply have to be accepted as part of working without a net.

Decision-making needs to be redefined as an exercise in risk management. We can no longer expect decisions where the outcome is guaranteed. Instead of yearning for the old risk-free days, it's time to adapt to the regret-free present. But what if a wrong decision might cost the company millions of dollars? What if a mistake might get me fired? How can anyone make such a decision without regret?

First, regret-free decisions aren't the same as foolhardy speculation or gambling. If the fate of an organization is riding on a decision, the decision maker better clearly understand and be prepared to deal with the consequences of failure. If a mistake is made, be ready to make another decision that might correct it or at least control the damage.

Second, if your boss will fire you for making one mistake, you don't want to be working for that boss. Any organization that is terrified of making a mistake is stagnant at best or heading out of business at worst.

FROM DECISIONS TO CHANGE

When you make a decision, you create change. Your circumstances naturally change because of what you've decided. If you decide to downsize your company, the company will never be the same again. But what stops many companies from making this decision—or making it too late—is a total misunderstanding of stress. When change is demanded, people go into stress. Unfortunately, we view stress negatively and try to eliminate it from our lives. In our downsizing example, one way of eliminating stress is not to downsize; to ignore the demand for change and maintain the status quo. Although this may temporarily eliminate stress, it may also permanently eliminate the company. If you postpone short-term stress, it doesn't change the fact that the company can't compete successfully unless it gets leaner.

Remember Paradigm 3 from Chapter 2: We need to change our attitudes toward change. Part of changing our attitudes involves changing our perceptions of stress.

In a high risk culture, people need to be in stress. Our society, however, has turned stress into the enemy, into something we should eliminate or at least reduce. Rather than viewing stress as a catalyst to growth, everyone from self-help writers to therapists sees it as unhealthy. In fact, just the opposite is true. Why do so many people die soon after they retire? Because they've stopped changing and being productive; they've removed all the stress from their lives. No decisions, no change, no stress, no life. The opposite of stress is not comfort and health; it's apathy and atrophy.

Instead of eliminating stress, we should get rid of distress—the inner turmoil that starts when our decision-making stops. While stress is a positive, activating force, distress is a negative, enervating one. Companies in distress can't respond to the demands of the marketplace. Like a fat and sleepy house cat that has had its natural instincts for survival dulled, the stress-free company is unable to rouse itself and respond to a marketplace shift. It is astonishing how quickly a distressed company can atrophy.

Exercise physiology provides another apt analogy. A number of studies of Olympic athletes revealed that after as few as seven days of not working out, their athletic condition deteriorated so quickly that it could take as long as a year to get back into peak shape. That is how fast the body atrophies, and the same is true for business. Stress prevents this from happening by forcing us to evaluate and reevaluate our decisions; to confront change. It keeps us alive and alert. Stress does not allow us the luxury of complacency. Stress is simply the state of mind and body created and resolved by decision-making.

Does this mean we can never sit back and enjoy what we've accomplished? Not at all. But it is terribly pessimistic to pose an either-or scenario: Either enjoy what we have or abandon it and go after more. We can enjoy what we have as long as we understand that we're going to want more. Our drive is to grow and learn, and that is what makes life interesting. Repeating the same behaviors is a nongrowth, nonlearning stance that causes individuals and organizations to shrivel up and die.

Organizations that are doing very well, however, sometimes subscribe to the opposite philosophy: If it ain't broke, don't fix it. In other words, why change and risk spoiling a good thing? Because it is a bigger risk to be caught unprepared when an opportunity or problem arises. Sooner or later, if the organization refuses to change, it will crash.

I'm not advocating change for change's sake. But all of us have a drive toward productivity and making an impact on people's lives. When individuals retire or organizations cling to the status quo, they cease to make a productive contribution. Embracing change mindlessly isn't the point; embracing it as a part of a larger process (the information cycle) is what's critical.

FROM CHANGE TO INFORMATION

Change exposes people to an entirely new base of information, returning them to the start of the information cycle. For example, an organization hears a great deal about total quality management. Based on that data, it has a number of choices related to bringing quality to its organization. It decides on a particular TQM approach and begins implementing it. Naturally, TQM profoundly changes the way the organization does business. A massive amount of new information pours into the organization from those changes. The company learns that its current computer system is not adequate for a company that aspires to quality goals. It realizes that it will have to reorganize the entire organization to make cross-functional teams more effective.

As this information pours in, choices are automatically posed about personnel, budgets, and so on. Decisions have to be made, which in turn leads to more change. The cycle keeps spinning. The quality movement offers us an excellent model to observe the information cycle in action, because its emphasis on continuous improvement dovetails with the information cycle's emphasis on continuous change and stress. Both have no endpoints, and both assume that things can always be made better.

HOW PEOPLE MAKE DECISIONS

Within this information cycle, decision-making is the key management tool. To use this tool effectively, we must understand how decisions are made. The following chart illustrates the underlying process.

The decision-making flow illustrated by this chart can be stated as follows: Decisions force us to prioritize, and when we prioritize, we're called on to determine what's most important to us, and to make that determination, we must know our core values.

That brings us back to one of the original paradigms: We should create value-driven personal and professional lives. Without values, regret-free decision-making is impossible. Training sessions, seminars, and conferences may teach people what to do, but without values, they lack the why. Without the why, they become victims of *chronically disabling ambivalence*. In other words, when faced with two choices, they respond, "Both of them seem to have validity." Or,

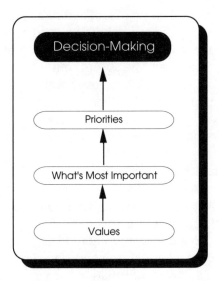

"I understand both points of view, I just don't know which one to choose." So they freeze; or if pushed to the wall to make a choice, they will second guess, reverse themselves, and regret the choice. Values will make the choice of options clear, and even if the results are disappointing, the decision won't be regretted.

We'll discuss value clarification and decision-making in much greater detail later. For now, remember that decisions can't be made in a value vacuum.

DECISION-MAKING CAN BE TAUGHT

The ability to make decisions rests on these attributes and tools:

1. Teaching professional skills and knowledge and providing personal and interpersonal insights
2. Creating opportunities for choices
3. Making decisions a necessity
4. Preparing comprehensively for change

1. Teaching professional skills and knowledge and providing personal and interpersonal insights

Most organizations do a fairly good job in the first area, helping their people develop and expand their skill and knowledge base. They realize that if employees don't know what to do and how to do it, they'll do nothing. When change is required, rather than making mistakes and being yelled at, such employees opt out of the decision-making process. They recognize they'll take less heat if they do nothing instead of doing something perceived as wrong or stupid.

But organizations often fall down in the second area. They don't help people understand who they are and how who they are affects others. When you don't realize how you affect other people, you can't be a good decision maker. For example, managers in technical positions within organizations frequently talk to nontechnical people without realizing they've lost their audience. That audience nods its collective head as if it understands, but the speaker's monotone and disorganization render his or her talk incomprehensible. As a result, any decision made by the audience from this point on is irrelevant—they're making decisions based on a flawed information base.

Multicultural companies exacerbate this problem. I recently worked with an organization where the head of its management of information service department spoke English as a second language. At a meeting, after listening to him speak, I said, "I have to tell you, I didn't understand a word you said." This is not a low-ranking "techie"; he is the person who controls the information flow for the entire organization. It turned out that no one else understood him either, and many poor decisions were made because of that lack of understanding. Why didn't anyone tell him that his English was bad? Because of the old caretaking posture that causes us to worry about offending others, no one told him.

In any organization, there are people who are unaware of the negative impact they have on others. It may be that Bill doesn't realize that his intimidating style forces his subordinates to make decisions solely to please him. Or Mary may be in the dark that her unassertive, uninvolved demeanor invites unproductive political game playing in her group. Bill, Mary, and everyone else won't make or help others make good decisions until they receive personal and interpersonal feedback.

2. Creating opportunities for choices

This can be done by avoiding caretaking. When we do things for others, we rob them of their choices.

But we can also create opportunities by delegating both authority and responsibility. Delegating one without the other doesn't work. If we say they're responsible for making decisions in a given area but insist that they clear every decision with someone else before they make it, that won't create opportunities for choices. We need to give our people the authority to take action and the responsibility for getting it done.

3. Making decisions a necessity

Hold people responsible for short- and long-term goals. Without goals, we can postpone our decisions indefinitely. With nothing to work toward, decisions are unnecessary.

Progressive discipline forces people to make decisions. By progressive discipline, I mean clearly communicating that there will be escalating punishments for failures to make decisions. For instance, if someone is consistently late to meetings and others respond with slight irritation or humor ("Some day Jerry will actually be here only five minutes late"), then the tardy attendee has no impetus to decide to get there on time. It is uncomfortable to tell that attendee, "If you keep arriving late to these meetings, you don't have to bother showing up at all." But the point of progressive discipline isn't to give people a hard time; it is to help them become decision-makers.

4. Preparing comprehensively for change

When change catches a company completely by surprise, employees respond by strategizing and making decisions in a crisis atmosphere. They'll do what is most expedient or they'll fall back on practiced behaviors rather than make new decisions. Organizations must brainstorm about how individuals and groups will react to change. If, for example, your company is going to launch a TQM effort, discuss which managers are most likely to be receptive to TQM and which ones are most likely to resist. You can determine which people will say, "I don't have time for this quality stuff, I have enough to do." For these people, you can choose from many tactics (workshops, one-on-one discussions, seminars) to co-opt them upfront.

Besides predicting reactions, planning responses is crucial. Knowing what to say in response to an employee's question about change can go a long way toward helping him or her deal with a new situation. Once you've predicted how people will react, you can plan a response that avoids the crisis mentality and panic that can accompany change.

TEACH YOURSELF HOW TO MAKE HIGH RISK DECISIONS

Though organizations can facilitate decision-making using the four aforementioned strategies, they can't make decisions for their people. Developing decision-making skills is necessary for survival in a high risk culture. To help develop those skills and capitalize on the information cycle, the following exercise will be useful. Though the focus of the exercise is on careers, the point is to help you become familiar with a new decision-making process. As you'll see, you can apply the exercise's methodology to any type of decision.

1. **List three options to your current career path.** These don't have to be feasible options—don't worry if you lack the time, money, education, or training to pursue them. It's okay if you're a secretary who wants to own her own business or a junior executive who wants to be CEO. In addition, other criteria for these options include

- Specificity. Writing that "I want a different type of job" is useless. Be as specific as possible about each career option.

- A reasonable time frame. Don't think about an option as something you'll exercise tomorrow. If you want to start your own business, you need to think about it as something that you'll do within the year and not the next day.

- Strong feelings. Your options shouldn't be careers or positions about which you're intellectually curious. They should be ones you're passionate to pursue.

2. **Prioritize your options.** But don't prioritize them in the traditional, intellectually rigorous, old paradigm manner. Instead

- Avoid asking the usual prioritization questions about each option, such as "Which one would my mentor advise me to choose?"; "What would make my spouse happiest?"; "Which one makes the most sense given my past experience?"

- Prioritize based on what you feel most like doing.

- If the three options are in a dead heat, pretend that someone is forcing you to number the options within a half hour, and you can't leave the room you're in until you do so.

3. **After you've identified the number-one choice, discard the other two.** You've just completed the most difficult task associated with decision-making: saying good-bye to other options. In many ways, this ability to discard is as important as the ability to identify choices. If you don't discard your options, they will surface and cause you to second guess your decision. The discarding process also helps you clarify your values, which we'll discuss in Chapter 10.

4. **Identify three changes in your life that this designated choice will bring about.** After you've written down those changes, prioritize each change from easiest to make to hardest. Circle the change that is easiest and cross out the other two. (As people become more experienced decision makers, I often reverse this step and ask them to discard the easier changes. For now, however, let's opt for the easiest one, because it will make the process less overwhelming.)

5. **Set a time frame for putting your choice into action that will result in the change described in Step 4.** Make a commitment to follow that time frame. Make your decision and take an action step (remember that this isn't an instantaneous process—what we're doing on paper might take weeks or months).

6. **What have you learned as a consequence of your decision?** How has that learning exposed you to a new set of choices?

As you've probably observed, this exercise allows you to trace the path of the information cycle. This exercise can be applied to any group of choices in your personal or professional life: from hiring options to acquisition alternatives to lifestyle choices. Repeating the exercise in various areas will enable you to improve your decision-making skills.

THE ONLY WAY OUT

Some people don't want to face these options. They want to escape the information cycle. The dizzying spin of the cycle throws them for

a loop. They can't handle the information overload, the many choices, the unending decisions, and the stress of change. If they look for
a way out, they'll find the exits shown in the following diagram.

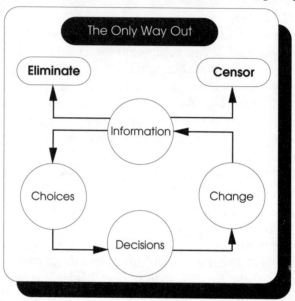

By eliminating or censoring information, you stop the cycle in its
rotation and may avoid choices, decisions, or change. For instance,
some organizations treat information as highly classified material
and provide access only to a select few. When employees ask, "Why
are we doing this?", managers respond, "Because the boss says so.
They don't tell me, so why would they tell you? Just do your job."
Other companies simply withhold information until it's too late to do
anything about it—for example, failing to tell employees that downsizing will be necessary until the pink slips arrive. In nonbusiness settings, two people embarking on a serious relationship fail to express
serious reservations about the other person until the relationship is
irreparably damaged.

Individuals and organizations that escape the cycle, however,
pay a high price. Although they may temporarily decrease the stress
in their lives, they also eliminate the rewards that come to people
who stay in the cycle.

It would be a mistake to underestimate the willingness of people to give up those rewards to avoid the cycle. Many seemingly inex-

plicable behaviors can be explained within the context of the information cycle. The chronically unemployed take themselves out of the agonizing (for them) decision-making process that comes with having a job—they don't receive the same quantity or quality of information when they're sitting at home. Similarly, those in a perpetual crisis mode at work are able to ignore decisions that would force them to orchestrate and organize their lives; they can seek refuge in the crisis mindset where there is simply no time to absorb information and consider the choices it presents.

The information cycle also goes a long way toward explaining the poor performance of otherwise bright and talented workers. When you perform poorly, your boss spends all his or her time talking to you about the mistakes you've made and how you must improve. Though hearing this might not be pleasant, it may be highly preferable to making decisions. You take yourself out of the cycle by performing poorly—you limit the information you receive, because no one wants to give new or challenging assignments to poor performers.

The cycle also explains why so many executives have problems with project management. Company after company complains that their people "just don't get it (project management)." It's not that they don't get it; it's that project management forces them to make decisions about how they work with other people. Acting as if they don't understand what project management is about takes them out of the cycle and helps them avoid those decisions.

These cycle escapes rarely occur at a conscious level—employees don't logically deduce that project management means new decisions regarding people, and therefore they will pretend they don't understand it. But just because this process occurs in the subconscious doesn't mean organizations are powerless to do anything about it.

Remember our new paradigm, "People's ability to change is not a function of capacity but of choice." How does management facilitate a choice to change?

Let's take a typical scenario. An employee is always in crisis—he never seems to have time to do what needs to be done and views every problem as an emergency. Typically, the reaction of management would be to send this dysfunctional employee to a time management seminar. But such a seminar doesn't get at the root of the problem. The following dialogue does:

> ***MANAGER:*** *What's the next position that you'd logically be promoted to here?*
>
> ***EMPLOYEE:*** *Assistant group manager. It would be my first supervisory position.*
>
> ***M:*** *Do you have any doubts about that?*
>
> ***E:*** *Not that I can think of.*
>
> ***M:*** *How would it affect your relationship with people you work with?*
>
> ***E:*** *Haven't thought about it.*
>
> ***M:*** *Do you think you could still be friendly with them?*
>
> ***E:*** *No, it would change things.*

The crisis mode employee is in this state to avoid confronting his feelings about bossing around his coworkers; he's terrified of the decisions called for if he became a supervisor. Contrary to what some people might assume, this employee is perfectly capable of managing without a crisis. But the crisis is an escape from the cycle, and only when the employee understands this fact can he deal with it.

This approach is far more effective than reeducation seminars or discussions with subordinates that misperceive the problem. I've known many managers who sit a poor performer down and ask him why he isn't performing up to his capabilities. It's like asking an 8-year-old why he hit his younger brother; if he knew why, he'd be practicing psychotherapy. To help poor performers get to the root of their difficulties, we have to find out why they feel the need to escape the information cycle and what prompted their escape.

Though I've focused on getting out of the cycle in work situations, people also try these escapes in their personal lives. Examples include drug and alcohol as painkillers for decision-making; psychosomatic illnesses, where people are relieved from making tough decisions because they're too "sick" to do so; and dead-end relationships that persist because the people involved are terrified of all the new choices, decisions, and change that would come when the relationship is over.

Whether the escape is professional or personal, the irony is that the only way out is destructive. The behavior of escapees is invariably dysfunctional.

WORKING WITH THE CYCLE (INSTEAD OF IT WORKING AGAINST YOU)

The information cycle explains many of the things that have gone wrong not only with individuals but with organizations and how those issues can be addressed. Think about how many organizations avoid change rather than embrace it. They are terrified by all the new information, choices, and decisions rolling toward them. They view the stress that accompanies change as unhealthy.

Looking at these issues from the perspective of the information cycle makes them less terrifying. For many people, the cycle is the first model that puts change and decision-making into a comprehensible context. There is a logic to the cycle and a clear benefit to be derived from it.

In a high risk culture, individuals and organizations that develop their decision-making skills have the opportunity to be more successful faster than ever before. But if those skills aren't developed, they will fail faster than ever before.

As valuable as these decision-making skills are, they must go hand in hand with relationship-building skills. We'll look at those skills in the next chapter.

CHAPTER

RELATIONSHIP BUILDING: MOVING FROM SCHMOOZING TO INTIMACY

Along with decision-making, relationship-building is one of the two critical skills essential for working without a net. As we saw in earlier chapters, people are the key to maintaining competitive advantage in an information-intensive, high risk culture. The unique skills of decision-making and relationship-building are all that can keep you on balance and moving forward. And a key part of moving from schmoozing to intimacy is to move from the old caretaking paradigm to the new caring for paradigm that was introduced in Chapter 2.

Two diametrically opposed models of relationship-building are shown on page 66. The old caretaking model is probably the more familiar one. With its emphasis on consensus, commonalities, and conflict-avoidance, it has been embraced by many organizations over the years. Its underlying premise is that the way to build strong relationships is to make other people feel comfortable and happy; that relationships are weakened when people become upset.

In an information-intensive culture, however, a caretaking stance is redundant. If all you do is tell people what they already

Caretaking

Old Model
Transactional

Consensus
Commonalities
Conflict Avoidance

Advantages

❐ Easier to initially implement.

❐ Usually results in a quicker payoff.

❐ Increases initial comfort and decreases initial tension in new situations.

Disadvantages

❐ Rewards plateauing and stagnation.

❐ Creates a mind-set of entitlement.

❐ Establishes a demeaning, hostile undertone.

❐ Leads to a need for revenge and retribution.

❐ Feeds denial and avoidance.

❐ Validates low self-esteem and low self-confidence.

Caring For

New Model
Relational

Challenge
Confrontation
Conflict Management

Advantages

❐ Encourages growth and development.

❐ Develops reciprocal, "equal" interactions.

❐ Communicates respect, builds self-esteem and confidence.

Disadvantages

❐ Harder to initially implement.

❐ Takes longer to produce results.

❐ Does not dilute initial discomfort and tension in new situations.

know and want to hear, you can be replaced by information technology—a computer can perform essentially the same functions.

The caring for model, on the other hand, allows you to use information to grow and develop people. By challenging existing beliefs and practices, you force people to explore new alternatives. You care enough for a client that you're willing to challenge her belief that Material A is best for her company. You care enough for a subordinate that you sit down and discuss how his failure to deal with his impending divorce has negatively affected his work. That deepens relationships in a way the caretaking stance cannot. It says that you're willing to devote time and energy to difficult issues that you could just as easily avoid.

To build relationships using the caring for model, four prerequisites or tools are necessary. Let's examine each of them and how they can lead to more productive, profitable relationships.

PREREQUISITE ONE: A HIGH DRIVE FOR GROWTH

High-growth people are most likely to build caring for relationships. They realize that no growth occurs outside of relationships; they will develop and maintain them in order to foster their growth.

Identifying people with high drives for growth can be difficult. For many years, organizations encouraged low-growth mindsets through their insistence that people repeat the same activities ad infinitum, believing that they would perform their jobs better through repetition. In fact, they plateaued and stagnated. Yet organizations rewarded people who were willing to repeat the same basic activities for years and didn't aspire to do something new or different.

People who have done well in low-growth companies probably are not the people you're looking for. To identify employees who will build relationships under the caring for model, differentiate between *self-initiating* and *reactive* contributions. Examples of self-initiating contributions include employees who come forward and say, "I need to be doing something differently" or "Have we thought about doing this project in another way?" They realize they may be putting themselves at risk with these statements (their boss may be an ardent supporter of the status quo), but their values will allow nothing less—they can't conceive of stifling their drive for growth, and it would make them crazy if they were forced to do so. This is as opposed to the reactive contributor who only responds when someone puts something on the table that elicits a comment.

To allow people with a high drive for growth to flourish, we have to establish norms that are the opposite of what training may have inculcated. For instance, we should tell our employees, "As soon as you've learned to do your job well, you should search for a new role or a way to do your job differently." Ask your superior for a new assignment or request a transfer to a different group.

These new norms can be clearly communicated to everyone in an organization. I have a client who, as a result of our work together, created a mission statement that was printed and sent to all employees. It told them that a new, key value of the company was, "We only want people working here whose goal is to outgrow their jobs."

Relationship-building and growth go hand-in-hand, and an organization should do everything possible to encourage the growth and development of its people. This growth and development is the company's rationale for existing. If it ceases to be its rationale, the company deserves to go out of business and it probably will. When no growth occurs, the company doesn't enter new markets or do anything better than it did before. The competition overwhelms them. But in an organization where the majority of employees have a high drive for growth, they will naturally form productive relationships that benefit both the individual and the organization.

Identifying high-growth employees—or spotting people with high-growth potential during the hiring process—is critical to the success of any company. To help you identify these people—and to separate low-growth from high-growth ones—I've created the following checklists.

HIGH-GROWTH TRAITS

- **Short learning curves.** These employees always astonish their bosses with how quickly they pick something up.

- **Boredom.** They become bored with repetitive tasks and aren't shy about saying so; they request new and different assignments to fight that boredom.

- **They regularly ask for help.**

- **They've tried a variety of things in their lives.** From a professional standpoint, this means they may have changed jobs and even careers more frequently than the norm.

- **A willingness to talk about their failures.** They have no problem talking about what they've done wrong as well as what they've done right.

LOW-GROWTH TRAITS

- **Long learning curves.** They seem to take forever to understand how to do an assignment and to complete it. These people aren't stupid; they worry that if they move too quickly, they'll be perceived as rushing through the assignment. These people also prefer to milk assignments and create the appearance that they're busy.

- **Everything is always fine.** They never admit to being bored. They're afraid to admit that things aren't perfect.

- **They only ask for help when they make mistakes.**

- **They rarely change jobs or careers.**

- **They never mention failures.**

Under the old paradigms, the traits on the high-growth list have been penalized. In the past, bosses have reprimanded employees who say they are bored and companies have viewed job-hoppers suspiciously. No more. The high-growth list validates behavior that is not only desirable, but is necessary for survival.

PREREQUISITE TWO: A CAPACITY FOR INTIMACY

I define intimacy as the ability to develop high-trust, closely bonded relationships quickly. The two critical skills here are self-disclosure and a willingness to engage in conflict.

Self-disclosure is not a goofy, confessional style of inappropriate candor but a high-trust posture that enables people to be resiliently open. The trust isn't so much in others as it is in oneself. In today's relationship climate, we need to be able to bounce back when we feel disappointed or betrayed. Without this capability, we won't form relationships because at the first hint of betrayal, we'll flee and isolate ourselves.

Let's say you're the owner of a widget-making company. A client makes a commitment to buy 4000 widgets from you. You begin production but then receive a call from the client, who says, "I'm sorry, but I can't go with the deal. I know I made a commitment to you, but I'm just too strapped for cash right now to honor that commitment." Without high self-trust, your response to this situation might be, "I'm never going to deal with a client like that again; I'm through dealing with small business types like him."

The high-trust response, on the other hand, would be, "I don't like getting burned, but I trust in my ability enough to pick up on the warning signs next time. I'm going to continue going after this type of client. Next time, though, I'll know better what to do and what not to do so I won't get myself in this type of jam."

The same high-trust, self-disclosing approach is necessary in relationships with peers, subordinates, and superiors. Low-trust postures, unfortunately, are common in corporations. A middle manager meets with a senior executive and discloses her desire to move up the corporate ladder, explaining that she feels very confident about her abilities and that they would be better used at a higher level. A month later, this middle manager is fired. She is terminated because, as one senior executive once told me, "When people come into my office telling me they want to do something different, I know they're going to look for another job, so I want to get them before they get me."

This middle manager has two choices. In her next job, she can close herself off and disclose nothing, assuming that if she was screwed once, she'll be screwed again. Or she can accept that there is a risk for self-disclosure, but a risk well worth taking. She can also learn from experience and become more discerning about who she trusts. High trust does not mean a Pollyannaish willingness to trust everyone. It does mean learning from one's mistakes and recognizing the limiting consequences of no self-disclosure. We're so disappointed when we're open with another person and they burn us that we develop a fortress mentality, eventually cutting ourselves off from new relationships and opportunities. High-trust people learn to handle this disappointment instead of constantly living in fear of it happening again.

WHAT'S YOUR TRUST POSTURE?

Are you and the people you work with self-disclosing and high trust? Affirmative answers to the following three questions indicate that you are.

1. **How comfortable are you talking about who you are to other people?** Self-disclosers explain to others who they are, not just what they do. No one builds relationships unless they reveal more than job-related facts. Contrary to the old paradigm—which held that others don't have the right to know about your personal life—the new paradigm says that it's a necessity that they know.

2. **Do you trust others?** In other words, do you feel that telling others about yourself will help relationships or be harmful to them?

3. **Are you willing to take risks trusting people?** Or, to put it in the context of an earlier point, would you tell your boss you were bored with the assignments he keeps giving you at the risk of earning his wrath?

THE ROLE OF CONFLICT IN TRUSTING RELATIONSHIPS

The other key skill in this relationship-building category is conflict. Contrary to what many of us have been taught, conflict is not a sign that a relationship is in jeopardy or might be destroyed. Conflict indicates that we've made an investment in people. Yet all too often, we see conflict manifest itself and immediately back off instead of pushing these feelings further to deepen the relationship. If we didn't care about the other person, we would go away—who needs the discomfort and aggravation that accompanies conflict?

You've probably noticed that we've come back to our new paradigm of caring for instead of caretaking. When you tell people what they need to hear instead of what they want to hear, you are trusting them to be able to deal with unpleasant truths. Conflict will arise, and it's important to maintain a caring attitude in the face of it.

Imagine having to tell someone who has been with your organization for 20 years that unless they start making a contribution, they will no longer be needed. That's devastating. The noncontributing employee will probably respond, "You must hate me to say something like that. After all this time and all I've done for this company, you really are ungrateful and unappreciative." If you're like most people, you'll reply, "I'm sorry, I didn't mean to hurt you. I hate to see you so upset. Forget what I said, don't worry about it."

This sends a destructive double message: You communicate the need for the employee to change, but you destroy the catalyst for change because you can't stand to see the employee so upset and hurt. A far more productive message would be to tell the employee, "I know you feel awful—maybe this is one of the worst things anyone has ever said to you here. But after investing all this time in the company, you're in danger of losing that investment because you haven't grown. I'd rather see you unhappy than throw it all away. So despite how awful you feel, I'm going to persevere and get into the details of what you need to do to grow, even though you keep telling me you don't want to hear about it." The manager who embraces this conflict cares far more about his employees than the one who can't stand to see any of his people unhappy and uncomfortable.

Relationships aren't meaningful unless you're willing to put them in jeopardy, and conflict certainly does that. But it does so in a constructive way, serving as a litmus test for relationships and helping you determine the truly worthwhile relationships in your personal and professional life. High risk people recognize that any relationship worth keeping is also worth walking away from.

PREREQUISITE THREE: HONEST AND DIRECT COMMUNICATION

Productive relationships are formed when people communicate based on their feelings, not just on their intellect. In other words, they rely on how they feel about a person and not just what a dispassionate analysis of that person tells them. Typically, businesses prioritize the head over the gut; they emphasize formal education over natural abilities and textbook strategies over relationships. But in my experience, people's feelings rarely betray them whereas their intellectual analysis betrays them at least half the time.

CEOs frequently talk themselves into business decisions and alliances even though their gut screams stop. When all the numbers add up and everything looks great on paper, they have trouble resisting what they instinctively know won't work.

Two major corporations I worked with merged a few years ago. On paper, the merger looked ideal, creating a synergistic blend of strengths. In reality, the companies' two cultures were diametrically opposed. One organization had a high-accountability culture; the other routinely indulged and encouraged employee excuse making. After the companies merged, there was chaos. People from the two companies could not work together and, in fact, grew to hate one another.

Top executives from both companies not only failed to identify the danger signals, but they denied those signals existed. We're so focused on "head" issues that we pretend that our gut feelings are somehow unreal and have no bearing on the *real* data.

THE INTUITIVE INTERVIEW

The capacity for honest and direct communication can and should be tested for in the recruiting process. This can be done in the following ways:

- **The unresolvable scenario.** Construct a situation that has no viable solution and present it to the interviewee. For instance, create a customer who is intractable—no one could possibly sell him anything. Then ask the interview candidate how she would deal with this customer. Some candidates will distort the situation to make a sale appear possible; they are the people who as employees will file reports that are more fiction than fact. What companies should look for are candidates who have enough trust in their own instincts to say, "I don't think this customer will buy in a million years." That is an honest and direct response, indicative of someone who can access her feelings and build relationships.

- **Inject conflict.** The interview process tends to be cozy and non-confrontational, filled with meaningless questions such as

"Why do you want to work here?" Instead, disturb the placid surface with a statement such as, "The last three statements you made contradict what you told me earlier this morning." Does the candidate become flustered and try to backtrack and cover himself? Or does he admit that the statements are contradictory? Some people panic and prevaricate when faced with conflict whereas others accept it and try and deal with it.

- **Tolerance test.** During the initial interview, refrain from mentioning anything about the company—nothing about salary, perks, working conditions, and so on. Focus on people and values issues. Determine how much tolerance the candidate has for nonhead issues. For example, if you are interviewing for a middle-management position, ask the candidate how she would handle high absentee rates, office rivalries, or insubordination. Does she seem uncomfortable and uncommunicative about how she feels relative to these issues? Does she try to steer the discussion back to things like salary and promotions? Or does she seem to relish talking honestly and openly about her beliefs and feelings?

PREREQUISITE FOUR: A TRANSITION FROM HIGH MAINTENANCE TO LOW MAINTENANCE RELATIONSHIPS

This fourth relationship-building skill is perhaps the most difficult one to attain, as well as the most important. In the past, we defined quality relationships in terms of time spent with other people (high maintenance). In the present, we're defining them as the level of intimacy established with others (low maintenance). By and large, we've done a pretty good job of making this transition in our work lives. The push of information has forced us to increase the number of relationships we enter but also to decrease the amount of time we spend on each interaction. The days of three-martini lunches are long gone. To survive, businesses have had to make the transition to low maintenance relationships.

If you doubt this, ask the following question of yourself or people you work with: When you get on the phone at the office, what's the first thing you want to do? Most people respond, "Get off!"

Because of our conscious or unconscious awareness of how valuable time is, we have shortened most interactions.

BLENDING OUR LIVES

We have not made the same transition in our personal lives. We have not done so because of the common assumption that if we don't spend a lot of time with people, we don't care about them. Our spouses berate us for working late three nights in a row, for missing a child's play, and for going out of town on business trips. Many new parents go back to work and aren't as productive because they're worried about what their work schedule is doing to their families. They're so preoccupied with their unhappy spouses or children that they can't concentrate on work. Or they tell their superiors that they can't work late again or go on that trip overseas because they'll burn out if they don't spend sufficient time at home.

In Chapter 2 we introduced this new paradigm: Who we are personally is inextricably connected to who we are professionally; the goal is to lead *blended*, not *balanced*, lives. Relationship-building skills must be blended into all parts of life to attain peak performance. Leaving them at the office results in burnout and frustration.

To develop low maintenance relationships at home, the key is to clarify what constitutes relationships with the important people in your life—to clarify the difference between schmoozing and intimacy. The former is a relatively mindless and emotionless exercise; the latter is a total emotional and intellectual involvement with another person. *Physical* attendance at all our child's plays, games, and other activities is not the same as *emotional* attendance; intimacy is achieved only when we are devoting our full attention to a particular relationship. Just because we are there doesn't mean we care. low maintenance relationships can be just as meaningful as high maintenance ones—more so, if the people involved stop going through the motions and start focusing on important issues.

The analogy here is to noncustodial parents. Simply because their interactions change from every night to every other weekend doesn't mean the relationship ends. The relationship will continue and grow as long as the parent is emotionally involved and open with the child when they're together.

Don't mistake this approach for the old "quality time" argument. As generally put forth, that argument posits that it's not the time you spend with someone that counts, it's the quality of time spent. As an example of quality time, proponents would trot out the example of a dad sitting down with his son and telling him what he did at work, or listening to what the child did at school. This exchange of facts, however, does not build relationships. Intimacy is produced through a sharing of feelings, not facts. The key is for the dad to tell the son how good it felt to clinch a big deal he'd been working on for months, and why it felt so good; or how sad he was when his father died and *why* he was so sad.

MAINTENANCE-LEVEL TEST

To identify high and low maintenance people, ask the following questions:

- **When you think about spending time with people you care about, do you think about allocating sufficient time or about what feelings you want to share with them?** The former indicates a high maintenance posture, and the latter a low maintenance one. If you're still not sure which category you fall into, follow up with these questions:

  In your conversations at work, do you find yourself reporting facts or sharing feelings?

  When other people share their feelings with you, do you try to redirect the conversation to what people do rather than how they feel about what they do?

For many managers I've worked with, making the transition from high maintenance to low maintenance personal relationships seems overwhelming at first. I've found that some key pieces of information make the transition more doable. Specifically,

- **Ask yourself if you assume that those closest to you are fragile.** In other words, do you assume that if you're not around, they'll fall apart? High maintenance attitudes are sustained by this notion of fragility. The odds are that neither your spouse, children, or close friend is fragile. Role play: Your boss says you are needed in an overseas plant for two weeks next month, and you're worried that your spouse will be furious if you miss her birthday and your wedding anniversary. Then ask yourself what is the worst thing that would happen if you were to go on the trip. Would your spouse kill herself? Would she have a nervous breakdown? Would she file for divorce? It's highly unlikely any of these events would transpire. We frequently maintain our high maintenance mindset because of our overblown sense of our own importance, not that of the significant people in our lives.

- **Find out the major goals of a person with whom you have a close relationship.** Any growth-related goals are fine. But if his or her major goal is to be propped up by you, not only will you be worn out, but the other person will be disabled. This person is saying he or she is resourceless without you around. Do you want someone you care about in a helpless, resourceless position? Of course not, which is why low maintenance relationships are necessary.

- **Define your responsibilities as husband, father, wife, mother, etc.** High maintenance people say that when they attempt a low maintenance approach, their spouses accuse them of "not living up to their responsibilities." The problem is failure to define the responsibilities you're willing and unwilling to take on and share that definition with others. For instance, one spouse loves reading to her children but despises rushing home from work to eat with her family. Her husband, on the other hand, relishes cooking meals and talking with his kids over dinner; he has never been a big fan of reading stories to the children at night, preferring to finish up paperwork after dinner. If each agrees on who does what, the wife can feel free to miss family dinners and the husband won't feel obligated to read stories to the kids at night.

  This isn't as hard nosed as it might sound. Neither parent can or should try to be all things to all people. When each allows the other to do what he or she enjoys and does best, each treats the other as a valuable resource.

  To facilitate the acquisition of the relationship-building skills discussed in this chapter, we need to keep our caring for model in mind. People get hung up on the concepts of low-maintenance relationships and honest, direct communication because at first blush they suggest harsh and unfeeling attitudes. In fact, just the opposite is true. Along with a capacity for intimacy and a high drive for growth, they embody a true caring for perspective.

C H A P T E R
THE
HIGH RISK
CULTURE

The relationship-building and decision-making skills discussed in the last two chapters are designed for a culture that may seem strange and unfamiliar. But it is real and affecting all our lives, no matter where we live or work. To pretend this culture doesn't exist is dangerous. Just going through the motions in the same old way can lead to disaster, and there's no net to catch you.

If you're not in sync with the change going on around you, your response will be late and down you'll go. Responding to change with fear and hesitation is as dangerous as not responding at all. To succeed in a high risk culture, you must be a person who can take risks.

Taking a risk measures the ability emotionally and psychologically to tolerate unpredictability, uncertainty, and vulnerability. Some people have a high tolerance for these factors, whereas others have a low tolerance. If you don't know what tolerance you have, you're in that gray middle ground where ambivalence causes hesitation. To understand the danger of this position and what a high risk culture entails, let's examine the high risk/low risk continuum from another perspective.

AUTONOMY VERSUS SECURITY

Low risk people possess a drive toward security. For them, security represents minimizing change and maintaining the status quo. Their outlook is pessimistic: *IF* things change, they will change for the worse. Similarly, they want the reassurance that what they have now is what they'll end up with.

high risk people, on the other hand, have a drive toward autonomy. They want to call the shots, to take control of their lives. Unlike low risk individuals, they don't want to control other people. They have no need to boss others around in a tyrannical fashion. Managers who manage by intimidation do so out of a low risk desire for security—if they can dominate the relationship by setting the terms, they ensure predictable behavior from subordinates. High risk people want to maximize the number and type of choices that come their way—the more choices, the more autonomy.

In the workplace, the low risk mindset translates into a desire for lifetime employment and a guaranteed paycheck. The high risk mindset seeks freedom and independence within a job. Though these people want to be held accountable for what they do, how they do it is up to them. They also desire performance-based compensation: They expect to be highly compensated for doing well and are willing to accept little or no compensation if they do poorly. In terms of jobs, low risk people gravitate toward teaching, law enforcement, and government work—careers that offer guarantees and security. High risk people are attracted to 100 percent commission jobs—sales and other positions where compensation is dictated by performance.

TRADE-OFFS

Just as it is impossible to be both high and low risk, we can't expect both autonomy and security. Trade-offs are necessary, and we should recognize the specific trade-offs when we choose a low- or high risk stance. In our society, examples abound of disenchanted individuals or groups who have failed to recognize the trade-offs dictated by their choices. Teachers, for instance, bitterly complain that they're underpaid compared to businesspeople given the social value of their job. In fact, teachers give up high pay when they choose a low risk, secure profession. Our culture rewards people for the risks they take, not for the perceived value (to society) of their choices.

There have been exceptions to this rule, most notably CEOs of some of our country's leading corporations. Though we have often rewarded people for risk as they ascend the rungs of the corporate ladder, we just as often abruptly stop doing so in higher-level decision-making positions. CEOs and other top managers receive the message that no matter how stupid their decisions may be, they'll be taken care of for the rest of their lives via golden parachutes, golden handcuffs, and other compensation. Is it any wonder that so many poor decisions have been made by so many executives in the past decade? Chief executives would function more effectively if their compensation more closely reflected their value to the company. In that way, they would have a significant incentive to make good decisions. Fortunately, CEOs are starting to get the message from their boards of directors that they won't allow them to become rich as their organizations decline.

CEOs, of course, aren't the only ones who have to come to grips with these trade-offs. We all have to define what's important in our lives. If we want a great lifestyle and all the options that come with it, then we had better opt for high risk and the concomitant financial rewards. This trade-off, of course, involves more than money. We are also choosing the challenge and discomfort that come with any high risk position.

BUT WHAT IF WE OPT FOR LOW RISK?

After assessing the trade-offs, some people might decide that low risk security is preferable to high risk autonomy. Although it may be preferable, it is not viable. Our culture is pushing everyone toward high risk and forcing us to abandon low risk. The reason: Low risk cultures will avoid conflict at any cost, and in that avoidance they create chronic problems.

Low risk people want everything to remain the same, and conflict raises the probability of things changing—the conflict between boss and subordinate suggests that the subordinate might have to leave (the department or the company). When we avoid conflict, real issues never get raised and problems never get solved. Look at the chronic problems in the workplace and society at large—violent cities, unemployment, low productivity. They continue because their solutions entail conflict. Cities remain unsafe because we refuse to set limits on outrageous behavior. Unemployment escalates because we deny that problems exist. Caretaking fosters a sense of entitlement that negatively affects productivity. We avoid potential solutions in each of these areas because they entail conflict.

Within a low risk organization, conflict avoidance leads to high turnover of the organization's best people. High performers become fed up with chronic problems that permeate these companies. They are worn down from watching management bend over backward to avoid conflict—these highly productive people leave meetings muttering, "If we go around that issue one more time, I'm going to go nuts." After a while, they leave the company. The same phenomenon exists in our political system. Politicians are so afraid of offending an interest group, even one making outrageous demands, that they avoid conflict by not dealing directly with the issues. Then problems are not solved, opposing groups become more polarized, and demands become more outrageous.

Similarly, highly productive people leave low risk organizations because they become fed up with equal rewards for unequal performance. They watch in disbelief as someone who produces mediocre work receives the same compensation as someone who works twice as hard and delivers more than twice as much value to the organization. As the saying goes, nothing is more unfair than treating unequals equally.

DOING BUSINESS IN A SHRINKING WORLD

We cannot avoid conflict in the 1990s even if we have done so successfully in previous decades. In a noninformation-intensive, nonconnected world, such a stance was possible. Companies in North Carolina could say, "People from New York make me nuts, so I'm just not going to deal with them." In a global culture, such isolation is no longer possible. The whole idea of a "local business" is an anachronism. The world's economy is interconnected. Your products and services are coming into direct competition with products and services all over the globe, whether or not that's your intent.

If you believe your company is immune to these forces—that it can continue to avoid conflicts raised by provocative and difficult people inside or outside your company—then consider the following anecdote.

For many years, factory managers in Eastern European countries bent over backward to avoid conflict. They never confronted suppliers of shoddy parts, even though those parts were responsible for frequent assembly-line breakdowns. In this caretaking atmosphere, managers were perfectly content to shut down the assembly line because they were paid no matter how poor productivity might be. When Western and Pacific Rim nations began opening factories in Eastern Europe, they were shocked to learn that the managers they hired refused to confront suppliers of shoddy parts. The new factory owners quickly disabused managers of their conflict-avoidance notions: If suppliers weren't able to provide quality parts, they ceased to be suppliers.

HOW WE AVOID CONFLICT

Conflict-avoidant behavior isn't always easy to spot; it takes on various forms that are viewed as acceptable in low risk organizations. To identify conflict avoidance in your company, watch for the following six manifestations or signs:

- **Denial.** As I've emphasized earlier, this is the number one problem in our country. In organizations, denial is in full bloom when a manager deals with an incompetent subordinate by saying, "Don't worry about it; just give him some time." People don't spontaneously recover from incompetence. Though confronting someone with his screw-ups isn't pleasant and will breed conflict, it's essential if you want the problem solved.

- **Relocation.** Instead of confronting problems, we move them around. Problem workers are transferred from one department or office to the next. Managers are promoted to positions and places where it's hoped they can do little or no harm.

- **Intimidation.** Bombastic, fear-inducing bosses earn reputations for thriving on conflict. In fact, they're terrified by it and try to stomp it out with their heavy-handed ways. If intimidators really embraced conflict, they wouldn't threaten their people to the point that they are afraid to voice a new or different opinion.

- **Inappropriate humor.** Everyone has heard conflict-avoiding humor. A CEO deflects a discussion about how poorly the company is doing by using black humor: "The bad news is that our quarterly results were down; the good news is that they can't get any worse." By treating a bad situation sarcastically or lightly, we avoid the core issue: The people who are working here aren't the right people to get the job done, or the way they're working isn't getting the job done.

- **Passive-aggressive behavior.** A common example is when someone promises you he'll complete an assignment but fails to do so. After repeated broken promises, you ask him why he hasn't done it and he says that he forgot. He didn't forget. The assignment raises the prospect of conflict, so rather than dealing with that conflict, he consciously or unconsciously uses his forgetfulness as a way out.

- **Co-opting.** Some people—especially those armed with MBAs—are experts at talking issues to death. They can create the illusion that they're tackling a tough issue head on, but what they're actually doing is disguising their inaction with verbiage. The conflict that would occur if they actually took action is avoided through talk.

SIGNS OF THE HIGH RISK SHIFT

Do we really have to jettison these conflict-avoidant behaviors now? Perhaps the high risk culture won't arrive for years; perhaps it will never arrive.

This wishful thinking is nothing more than another way to avoid conflict. Consider the following six signs that a high risk culture has arrived.

- **Job fluidity/mobility**. According to government and private sector studies, people who entered the job force around 1980 will have experienced five to seven job changes and three to five career changes by the time they're ready to retire. This is evidence of the uncertainty and unpredictability that pervades our culture.

- **Growth in self-employment.** The growth in the last decade of small- to medium-sized businesses outnumbered big corporations by a 15 to 1 margin. We're seeing many more people deciding to work for themselves rather than for others. Autonomy has taken precedence over security.

- **Increased competition.** As the information cycle shows, information catalyzes intense competition on local, national, and international levels.

- **Greater focus on accountability.** In companies throughout America, the competition creating our global economy forces people to pay more attention to issues of productivity. In such a global economy, accountability is necessary to survive, let alone prosper.

- **Emphasis on self-marketing.** With the old mindset of "jobs for life" disappearing, people are much more focused on selling themselves. Self-marketing was a relatively low priority in the old low risk days, because few people moved from company to company and career to career as they do today. Two signs of this trend are the proliferation of self-help books and tapes and the explosion of career counseling services.

- **Transition from credentials to experience.** In a low risk culture, companies are obsessed with credentials such as advanced degrees (the MBA mentality) and previous employers (the more prestigious the company, the better). The shift here is to a more pragmatic evaluation—what skills have you acquired and what can you do specifically for us? A sign of this shift can be seen in the types of questions interviewers are now asking. Instead of requesting a list of degrees obtained and companies worked for, they want to know what candidates have done successfully.

IDENTIFYING HIGH RISK PEOPLE

Are you a high risk person? What about the people you work with and who work with you? Certain traits or behaviors are indicative of high risk individuals. The following two checklists will be helpful in the identification process.

HIGH RISK PROFESSIONAL CHARACTERISTICS

- Direct communicator

- Quick decision maker

- Effective and efficient listener

- Delegates responsibility and authority

- Views mistakes as learning experiences

- Sets clear and unambiguous performance expectations

- Utilizes conflict and confrontation as problem-solving options

- Delivers immediate and consistent rewards and consequences

HIGH RISK PERSONAL CHARACTERISTICS

- Great reliance on instinct

- Self-disclosing and interested in others

- High curiosity/need to learn and explore

- Capacity to generalize from the particular and to take action

- High regard for self-approval

- Low need for consensus and universal approval

- Driven by intrinsic motivation

PAYING THE PRICE

If you embrace the behaviors and attitudes of the high risk individual, you need to understand your decision within the context of stress and distress. Low risk people exchange short-term stress for long term distress. High risk people are constantly under short-term stress and rarely experience long-term distress. When you strike a low risk posture, you may avoid day-to-day stress, but you accumulate unmade decisions that ultimately cause you much unhappiness. High risk people, on the other hand, constantly make decisions and face change-related stress, but they never look back on their lives with regret. High risk people regularly pay a price for being successful in this culture, whereas low risk people avoid paying until a big amount is due at some point down the road. It's the difference between making fixed payments on a loan and a gigantic balloon payment after a period of time. In a high risk culture, no one can afford to accumulate such a huge debt and expect to be happy or successful.

PART TWO
GROWTH AND SUCCESS

CHAPTER

GROWTH AND SUCCESS: HIGH RISK MODELS AND TOOLS

In the previous chapter, we examined the process of making decisions in a high risk culture. Of course, these decision makers are not functioning in a vacuum, but within a corporate structure. Corporations must facilitate the ability of employees to work without a net. Even the most agile new-paradigm managers will be hamstrung by a corporation that undermines its risk takers and rewards old-paradigm behavior.

In this chapter, we will look at the sort of structure a corporation must have to enable new-paradigm behavior. I provide a diagnostic tool for locating the problem spots in any corporation and suggest exercises to correct the problem.

Before I discuss these tools and exercises, let me clear up a common misconception. Because of my use of the term *high risk*, people frequently assume that I'm advocating an entrepreneurial approach; that in a high risk culture, the only acceptable model is the risk-taking, entrepreneurial one.

In fact, just the opposite is true. Entrepreneurial models are fatal to growing, successful companies, whereas corporate models facilitate and sustain success and growth.

What I'd like to do here is help you understand why this is so and provide you with information and tools to implement a corporate model that will function effectively in a high risk culture.

ENTREPRENEURIAL VERSUS CORPORATE

The entrepreneurial model is predicated on small size and high control. The corporate model is based on large size and high delegation. Although an entrepreneurial approach is constructive for start-ups, it is destructive when companies begin to grow. When people launch companies, control is essential and relatively easy to maintain—essential because one wrong move can kill a venture before it gets off the ground and relatively easy because most start-ups don't have many employees. When an organization takes off, however, the number of employees increases and it becomes progressively more difficult for management to control all these people.

Yet most organizations view the entrepreneurial model as positive and preferable to the traditional hierarchical corporate structure. It seems more in tune with the call for flattened, delayered companies.

But an entrepreneurial model is actually a classic example of functional pathology: It's functional for the context it's in, but take it out of that context and it's pathological. In other words, within the context of a start-up, entrepreneurial management is functional; if the company were never to grow, it would remain functional. But as soon as the context is removed—when growth and success come—the pathology sets in.

Airline pilots provide a good analogy. They are trained to be functionally pathological—to operate with analytical clarity and without feelings. If they were to start worrying about how their passengers and crew are feeling during a difficult maneuver, they would probably crash. That's why they are so calm and collected even when their landing gears won't deploy, engines are on fire, or fuel is leaking. The problem occurs when the context shifts— when they go home to their families and that new environment renders their cool, dispassionate demeanor dysfunctional. Individuals who share no emotions with their families have serious problems.

The same thing happens to entrepreneurs whose companies have grown. They have lost the context where control is necessary or possible. Although entrepreneurs are high risk types financially, they are low risk emotionally and psychologically. They are unable to abdicate control and delegate. There are entrepreneurial CEOs who employ 5000 people but still run their businesses like the corner deli. They say to their employees in word or deed, "I want you to do everything exactly the way I do." This micromanagement approach prevents people from investing in their own growth and development. In this situation, entrepreneurial managers are classical low risk caretakers.

Contrary to popular belief, the corporate hierarchical model is not outmoded. In fact, the high degree of structure it provides is absolutely necessary. When organizations grow, the pyramid model facilitates the process of giving up control. Its multiple, connected layers make extensive delegation possible and it also fosters accountability. The traditional pyramid structure is more valid today than ever before, particularly when managers stop caretaking and employ the caring for paradigm. Growth only occurs in hierarchical structures; it doesn't take place in flat ones.

The criticism often leveled at hierarchies has nothing to do with the essential structure and function of the pyramidal model. These problems all come from one source—conflict avoidance. Hierarchies become dysfunctional when decision makers don't want to confront redundancy and incompetence and instead bury the problems in another organizational layer. Or they find it too painful to confront difficult but key people who use legitimate roles and functions in illegitimate, destructive ways. Hierarchies don't do damage to businesses any more than alcohol creates problem drinking. Structures don't create problems; people do.

ENTREPRENEURIAL TRAITS

You can evaluate your organization's entrepreneurial tendencies by determining if top management manifests the following characteristics:

- **Tries to control people.** In their quest for complete control over the lives of their subordinates, caretaking managers unknowingly demean their people, robbing them of self-

respect and creating tremendous hostility and resentment.
They tell people how to perform tasks rather than what needs
to be accomplished. They try to orchestrate every aspect of
work life and overreact to any action that causes conflict. A
structure that enables delegation also enables employee
growth and shows people what they need to do to succeed. A
flat, controlled structure has no paths for growth, and success
becomes whatever keeps the boss happy.

- **Tries to control information.** When managers deny employees
  important data, they take them out of the information cycle.
  Typically, entrepreneurial managers adopt the following attitude toward their people: "I'll tell you what you need to
  know, but you make the decision." Without sufficient information, however, employees make dumb decisions. The
  entrepreneurial managers then yell at the employees, asking
  "Why did you make such a stupid decision?" The answer, of
  course, is because those managers hoard information like
  gold.

- **Juvenile delinquent personality.** Like savvy teenage rebels,
  entrepreneurial managers are smart and opportunistic, but
  also untrusting and suspicious. They seem to have eyes in the
  back of their heads—they don't miss a thing that's going on in
  the organization. But subordinates feel these managers don't
  trust them to do anything on their own.

PINPOINTING THE PROBLEM: A DIAGNOSTIC TOOL

When an entrepreneurial model is used, organizations invariably
experience a wide variety of problems—from managers who are
unwilling to compromise to conflict-avoidant employees. To deal
with these problems, the following six-stage developmental
process model will be helpful:

Let me briefly explain how this process works. Everything
starts with trust, and your ability to trust dictates your attitude

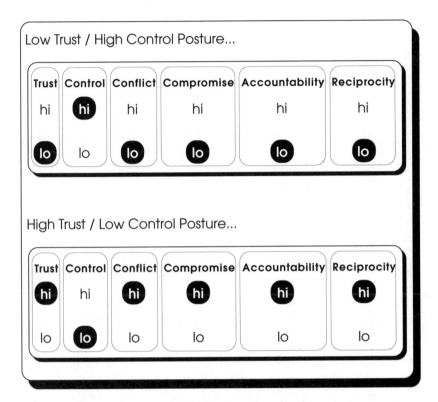

Low Trust / High Control Posture...

Trust	Control	Conflict	Compromise	Accountability	Reciprocity
hi	**hi**	hi	hi	hi	hi
lo	lo	**lo**	**lo**	**lo**	**lo**

High Trust / Low Control Posture...

Trust	Control	Conflict	Compromise	Accountability	Reciprocity
hi	hi	**hi**	**hi**	**hi**	**hi**
lo	**lo**	lo	lo	lo	lo

toward change. High-trust people are low control—they trust others sufficiently that they're not concerned that they don't know what every employee is doing at every moment of every day. Low-trust people, on the other hand, are high control. Moving one stage down, high-control people are low conflict, whereas low-control people are high conflict. Starting with conflict through the last three stages, the correlations cease to be inverse. For instance, high-compromise people are also high accountability—your ability to compromise allows you to negotiate expectations and consequences for which you hold others accountable.

Both individuals and organizations develop along these six stages. Under the entrepreneurial model, however, problems can develop in any of these stages and inhibit development. Growth and success depend on decreasing control and increasing trust, and entrepreneurial management prevents this.

If you're experiencing a particular problem in your work environment, try the following exercise:

Identify a specific problem within your organization and then pinpoint that problem as one of the six stages. To find the source of the problem, move one stage back. There you'll find the developmental issue your organization needs to address. Here are some examples:

- Someone in the organization says, "Relationships here are a one-way street; some people get everything they want, while others get nothing." This problem can be located in the reciprocity stage. But it's the stage above it—accountability—that's causing the problem. When no one is held accountable for their actions, it's impossible for equal and fair relationships between employees to exist.

- People complain that "no one around here does what we need them to do." You locate the stage as accountability and the source of the problem as compromise. People have not gone through a process of negotiation and commitment to shared goals and values.

- If you find that everyone in the organization is "rigid as hell" and that "no one negotiates anything," the locating stage is compromise, and the cause of the problem is conflict (or, more exactly, low-conflict attitudes).

STARTING AT THE TOP: A REMEDY

As organizations use the six-stage developmental process to pinpoint the source of their problems, they find themselves moving back up to the first stage of the process: trust. Increasing trust levels is crucial for growing, successful organizations, and to do so requires giving up control and taking risks in relationships. The following exercise will help everyone within an organization increase his or her trust level:

Choose a work relationship where not much is on the line—a secondary vendor, someone in another department with whom you have infrequent contact. Address an issue you've never addressed with that person before, an issue you've dodged. Maybe it's his inability to communicate his points effectively in large meetings or a tendency to be closed off and impersonal. Whatever it is, set a time and place and discuss the issue with the other person. After the meeting, think about what just took place: You and the other person survived the discussion. Next time, repeat this exercise, only this time choose a relationship where there is more on the line. As you escalate the risk level, you're increasing your trust level.

OTHER EFFECTS OF SUCCESS AND GROWTH

Some organizations shed or never embrace the entrepreneurial model yet still encounter problems as they grow. Even if your company is low control and high delegation, relationships will change and personal accessibility will diminish as the company grows. As companies add people, open new offices and factories, and move to bigger, larger office space, the common complaint is, "This company is getting too big. It's no longer a family and is just like every other business. People I used to talk with every day I now have to make appointments to see. No one has time for me anymore."

Organizations rarely deal with problems produced by decreasing personal accessibility. Let's look at the two main issues raised by decreasing accessibility and what organizations can do about them:

- Clear choice points at work.

- An increased focus on life outside of work.

CHOICE POINTS

When people find that others in the organization have less time for them, they question what they're doing there. It is obviously no longer the same organization that they joined years ago, and growth and change raises choices: Should they stay or should they go?

But when employees go into their managers' offices and say, "I really don't know why I'm here anymore," managers often respond, "Don't say that. Of course we need you, don't even think about leaving."

A far more effective managerial response in a growing company would be, "You're absolutely right. This organization has grown and placed different demands on all of us. You should think about whether you want to be here. It may be that a better place for you is a start-up organization where you get to talk to the boss every day."

The following exercise will help you gauge your reaction to decreasing personal accessibility:

> *Think about what has happened in the past when someone came into your office to talk to you about his dissatisfaction with work. Was your response to try and talk him out of his dissatisfaction? Or did you ask what dissatisfied him and encouraged him to make a choice about his current situation?*

In growth companies, encouraging people to talk about the choices facing them is the best thing managers can do both for their people and their organizations. It may well be that they are in the right place. But the autonomy and responsibility that comes with change and growth scares them. As a result of their fear, they assume that the problem is "outside"—the company has become too big. Instead, it's inside, and by talking about it, they can face the biggest growth challenge of their lives.

INCREASED FOCUS ON LIFE OUTSIDE OF WORK

In growing organizations, an individual can't get personal needs for affiliation met to the same extent that he or she can in stagnant organizations. Coworkers and superiors no longer have time to tell him what a great guy he is or to listen to him talk about his great weekend or to talk him through his divorce. Most of the time people spend together at work now revolves around business matters.

For employees of growing, successful companies, personal lives have to provide greater levels of satisfaction. Yet they frequently do not. One of my clients was an accounting firm that grew by leaps and bounds. The hardest-working partner in the firm was a single guy who had never been involved in a meaningful personal relationship. He worked like a dog; his work was literally his life. But as the firm grew, he became the first casualty. The other partners no longer had time to sit down and just talk with him. The people who worked for him no longer were in his office every second asking what to do next; the firm had delegated more tasks to each person and everyone was encouraged to operate with greater autonomy. The hard-working partner couldn't handle these changes and left the firm.

To avoid losing a talented and productive person, this man's partners could have confronted him and said, "You're forty, and you have absolutely nothing going on in your personal life." But they avoided the conflict such a confrontation would produce.

As a manager in a high-growth company, you can increase the odds of retaining valuable employees who say, "I don't like it around here anymore." Instead of sympathizing with them and agreeing that the growing bureaucracy is no fun, ask the following questions:

- Where are you getting your personal needs met?

- When you do a good job, do you find that simply being told you did a good job isn't satisfying; do you resent that no one tells you what a great person you are for doing a good job?

- When you go home, do you have a relationship that affirms that you're a great person?

This goes back to our new paradigm of the blending of personal and professional lives. People whose personal and professional needs are met enjoy going to work and going home, and they have little or no problem integrating the two.

Although all this holds true for employees regardless of title, it becomes increasingly relevant the higher up the corporate ladder you go. As you move up through the ranks of a high-growth company, you receive less and less personal validation. The higher you go, the more isolated you become—the isolation caused by decreasing commonalities and the necessity of making tough decisions (a CEO who is close friends with scores of employees has a harder time making a downsizing decision). Your interactions with others are shorter, and you're delegating more than ever before. In addition, the higher you go, the fewer people there are above you to whom you can confide your fears and problems (confide in subordinates and they'll wonder if you're losing your grip).

Top executives need strong personal relationships to receive the validation that is in short supply at work.

THE DILEMMA OF
DEVELOPING SUCCESSFUL PEOPLE

Successful, growing organizations naturally produce successful, growth-oriented people. Though this is the logical product of the corporate model, there is also a byproduct: The more you develop successful people, the more autonomy and fewer constraints they want in their professional lives. The challenge for organizations is meeting these escalating needs. Sometimes the most successful employees outgrow the corporate growth curve and leave the organization. The irony is that sometimes a company's best people leave because the company has done such a good job in developing them.

If your organization is facing this situation, here are two viable responses:

1. Demand that everyone in the organization grow, not just a select group. Companies that "protect" certain people from growth drive down the organizational growth curve and drive out the people who are growing the most; these people resent the organization's unwillingness to confront individuals who have plateaued and how it prevents the organization from reaching its potential.

2. Learn how to "let go" of successful people. Sometimes highly successful individuals need to leave organizations and seek greater autonomy in other jobs or by starting their own businesses. Perhaps your company won't or can't provide the freedom from constraints they seek. In that case, let them go. Entrepreneurial managers struggle with this concept; they have difficulty letting go of anything, especially people they've invested a great deal of time, money, and energy developing. They see their departures as betrayals. They ask the departing employee, "How can you leave after all I've done for you?" Rather than feeling betrayed and regretting the loss, organizations should focus on escalating their growth curve, knowing that they will keep the majority of their best people if the curve is high.

HELPING EVERYONE
MAKE THE TRANSITION

The segue from entrepreneurial to corporate model won't come without some head scratching and protests. Some employees will be confused or angered by a high risk management model. To help your people deal with three of the most common issues raised by the new model, consider the following steps:

1. **Encourage managers to practice letting-go behaviors.** Entrepreneur-managed companies usually include many people who are trying to do everything; they want to control as much of the work as they possibly can. This delegation exercise will help managers make the transition to an environment of decreased control. Have your people create a list of their skills and talents, and then compose another list of all the tasks they take on. Have them compare the two lists and see what tasks are unrelated to skills and talents. They can then delegate the unrelated tasks to others.

2. **Prepare people for the unexpected.** Small-group meetings can preview the unexpected aspects of change, such as less time for personal interactions at work. These meetings should not revolve around technical changes such as new job responsibilities. They should clearly communicate that a growing company will change how employees relate to others. Meetings should also allow employees to think and talk about if they want this change in their lives and if they're ready to deal with it.

3. **Shatter the myth that workers should keep personal problems to themselves.** As I've emphasized, the first people to go in growing, successful companies are people whose personal relationships (or lack thereof) are not meeting their needs. The old work taboo prohibiting discussion of sensitive, emotional issues can't be maintained. Top management should make it clear that no one will be penalized because they have or share their problems; top managers should also make it clear that people will be penalized if they don't deal with those problems.

C H A P T E R

INDIVIDUAL GROWTH AND SUCCESS:LEARNING TO COPE WITH LOSS

We've been talking about taking risks, letting go of control, and enabling change instead of resisting it. This is difficult on a corporate level, but it's also difficult on a personal level. An individual can soon find himself or herself flying faster and higher than is comfortable. It can be frightening to work without a net.

Some employees who begin to succeed in a high risk culture are soon unsettled by the experience. Discomfort causes people to pull back, slow down, perhaps even sabotage their own careers to avoid the stress of change. This chapter will concentrate on what happens to individuals who succeed and how they can save themselves (and their coworkers) from self-destruction.

WHAT WE GAIN
AND WHAT WE LOSE

Personal success is widely misunderstood because we associate it only with the overt gains and not with the covert losses. The following gains are familiar to most of us:

- Goal achievement

- Personal satisfaction

- More money

- Greater status

- Better lifestyle

But we also lose:

- Friendships and support groups

- Occupational or professional identity

- Personal, family, and subcultural identity

To understand how this loss occurs, begin by thinking about the similarities between success and loss. Both are profoundly life-altering experiences, resulting in redefinitions of self, others, and relationships. When individuals succeed at work, they are no longer the same person who struggled to get a job done. By getting the job done, they have surpassed everyone's expectations, including their own.

For example, Joe used to think of himself as the most inexperienced, least skilled assistant product manager in the organization. But when he was responsible for one of the company's most successful new product introductions in its history and received kudos from top management, he automatically redefined his identity within the company. The neophyte, uncertain, junior employee he once was disappeared. *He lost his occupational identity.*

Not only is the self redefined by success, but so is one's view of others. Think of a boss or mentor who you greatly admired early in your career. When you were just starting out, she seemed brilliant and enormously talented. But with your success came a startling realization: she was just average. The more you achieved, the less brilliant your boss or mentor became.

Further, success redefines relationships. It creates different expectations and produces different needs and demands. Relationships are no longer viewed in the same light, as the following example illustrates.

Susan is a very bright, talented person who started out in a clerical position. But it is clear to management that she has all the tools to be a star. They sit down with Susan, tell her that she has what it takes to move up in the organization, and ask her if she's interested. Susan says "Of course." Her supervisor says that the company will develop her, send her to seminars, and generally place her on the fast track that leads out of clerical and into management.

But no one addresses the impact of this fast track on Susan's relationship with her husband. Herman is a television repairman who has certain expectations of Susan; he expects her home before he arrives, for dinner to be on the table, for his wife to keep her work life confined to weekdays, nine to five.

If Susan accepts her promotion and she continues to grow and develop, one of three things will happen:

1. Susan will rapidly tire of Herman's rigid demands and the relationship will end.
2. Susan's growth will goad Herman to grow, and he'll no longer be content with his life as a TV repairman or stone-age husband. He'll be willing to negotiate time and other relationship issues with Susan, and he'll want to own his own business or pursue another direction that will allow him to develop.
3. Susan will sabotage her growth to stay with Herman.

It's this last action that occurs most often. People turn down or sabotage growth opportunities to preserve their current relationships. Consciously or not, they recognize that if they accept a promotion or fast-track opportunity, their relationships will never be the same again. In our example, Susan might tell her supervisor, "I've thought about your offer to go into management, and I realized it's just not for me." (Or she might accept the position but fail to work up to the level expected of her.) What she really would be saying is, "There's too much loss here."

The only way for management to prevent Susan—or anyone in this position—from sabotaging her success is to point out the challenges and potential losses of growth and discuss these issues with her.

LOSING THE FAMILIAR

When you're successful, you're guaranteed to have new and different experiences all the time. Failure, on the other hand, returns you to what you know, to the familiar. When people find themselves frightened by all these new experiences, they sabotage their success to slow it down.

For instance, an entrepreneur starts a business, it takes off, and he's faced with a demand from new markets for his service. But he started his business to serve one market—perhaps a business segment he had dealt with before he became an entrepreneur. Suddenly, his success requires him to deal with a host of new people. He may be subconsciously thinking, "Hey, I'm just an average guy from the wrong side of the tracks who got lucky. There's no way I'm going to be able to deal with these slick operators from the *Fortune* 500 companies." So rather than confront the unfamiliar and the uncomfortable, he doesn't return calls from these prospective customers or he is rude or unhelpful when he talks with them. This sabotage returns him to his old, familiar customer base.

The same thing happens with up-and-coming managers who seem to hit the wall suddenly. A manager experiences a steady rise through the ranks and then, for no apparent reason, his performance slips. He turns in reports late, misses a crucial meeting, makes a rookie mistake with his quarterly forecast. It's inexplicable, and everyone in the organization says there must be something wrong. There is, only it's not what everyone thinks. This manager doesn't want to lose the familiar—the routine of his middle-manager job, the coworkers he has become friends with—so he sabotages his success.

LOSS OF ROOTS

Success threatens to create a gap between who we were raised to be and who we might become. To take the most extreme example, consider what happens to someone who grew up in poverty and has become a highly successful businessperson. His family is uneasy with his success. They believe he spends his money extravagantly and can't understand how he could spend $40,000 for a car and $500,000 for a house. They resent that he doesn't like visiting the old neighborhood anymore. They are upset that he has new friends whose backgrounds are foreign to the family's. They disparage many of the trappings of success, telling him that he's changed and that success has gone to his head.

Feeling as if he has to choose between his family and his success, this rags-to-riches man may choose his family by sabotaging his success. Subconsciously, he may blow a few deals or alienate customers and superiors to bring himself down to a level more acceptable to his family. We see this scenario played out in public by lottery winners and celebrities. The fame and fortune they receive alienate them from the cultures in which they were raised. They frequently feel lonely and isolated; there is a gap or loss because they have become much different from what their backgrounds told them they would be. The lottery winner may start giving away his money or lose it in a series of incredibly stupid investments; or the famous athlete may self-destruct through gambling, drugs, and alcohol.

In business, I've witnessed an especially acute problem involving minorities in sales positions. When they do well, their cultures frequently try to slow them down. Immigrants, for instance, find that their sales success accelerates the assimilation process, pushing them farther away from their roots. They lose their accents, they stop going to the immigrant group's social functions, they move out of the ethnic neighborhood. Most significantly, they view and relate to their families differently. Their families then send them messages: "Who do you think you are?" The fear of losing their families, their roots, ends up catalyzing some form of sabotage.

Why do families impose these feelings of guilt and loss on their offspring? Don't they want them to do well? Yes and no. Families raise children with two agendas. First agenda: We want you to succeed and have a better life than we did. Second agenda: Just don't do that much better. The subconscious motivation for that second agenda is that if children do too well, they move away from the family (geographically and psychologically). They will no longer have as much in common. Moderate success, therefore, is much preferred to great success.

For example, I work with the head of an organization who is one of the brightest, most talented people I've ever met. Yet both he and his company have been plateaued at the same level of production for years. He acknowledges that he should be doing better and that he'd like to make more money. But his background won't allow him to take the risks necessary to move to the next level of success. He is unable to go to the bank and obtain a loan that would fund his company's expansion. He is unable to do so not because he thinks expansion is ill-advised, but because he was raised in an environment where debt was a sin. His father always paid cash, and his dad's philosophy was, "If you can't afford it, don't buy it."

THE LOSS OF NECESSARY LIMITS

Success threatens to push us into chaos. The familiar parameters of a job that we've probably done long and well suddenly vanish. The goals that we've been shooting for—goals that gave structure and direction to our lives—no longer exist once they've been reached. In their absence, we face a dilemma: to go through the demanding process of setting new goals/limits that will invariably plunge us back into chaos once we've reached them or to sabotage our success and return to old limits and old goals.

The following chart illustrates this dilemma:

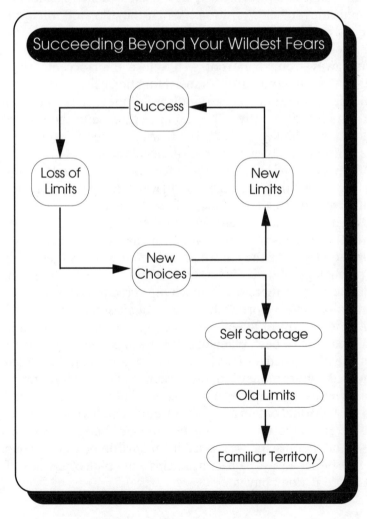

Faced with the loss of limits, many newly successful people opt for the self-sabotage path of the chart. Threatened with potential chaos and establishing new goals and limits, they choose to work on the same things all their lives—they remain in the same job (or type of job) repeating the same tasks that they mastered years ago. Achieving goals is not always the unambiguous positive that such accomplishments are perceived to be. Instead, the accomplishments make people feel disorganized and insecure, because the organizing goals they depended on for so long are no longer around. The self-sabotage path, on the other hand, offers people the security they desperately seek.

THE FUNCTIONING OF GOALS

The attraction to limits that are established by goal setting should not be underestimated. Goals serve the following three roles in our lives:

- They teach us that we can effectively manage our feelings and emotions.

- They reassure us that we will not overwhelm ourselves with our own impulses and desires.

- They give us external constraints to reinforce our internal constraints.

People often think the sole purpose of goals is to establish a destination to move toward. But they also set the limits described in the three aforementioned roles, and that's what adults find so attractive about goals. In the same way that discipline establishes safe boundaries for children, goals impose limits on adults that foster feelings of safety as they move toward their destinations.

But when we reach our destinations—when we achieve our goals—we're most vulnerable to failure. We become caught up in celebrating our achievements and neglect to reset new goals for ourselves. Without that resetting, chaotic feelings descend and push us toward safe, no-risk paths. That's why we need to impose limits and constraints continuously or we'll be vulnerable to failure.

HOW TO KEEP
CHOOSING NEW LIMITS

Every successful individual in every organization needs to learn how to handle the continuing losses he or she will face. Unless you're able to recognize the losses for what they are and work through them, you'll find yourself returning to old, familiar goals and limits. This step-by-step action plan will help you deal with loss and facilitate choosing new limits.

> *STEP 1. Create a list of major things you no longer have in your personal and professional life that you had ten years ago. What have you lost in terms of relationships, career or job options, and responsibilities? Next to each thing lost, write the cause of that loss. For instance, "Less hands-on responsibility for getting jobs done—cause: promotion to top management level."*

The point of step 1 is to learn how to identify losses. This step helps people understand the connection between success and loss. It also gives them a sense of how the loss took place. Let's say your loss is that you have less time for college friends and work buddies, and the cause of that loss is marriage and dual careers.

Your losses aren't negative. They are simply the logical consequence of specific life choices. But if you don't acknowledge and grieve those losses, they'll sabotage any further growth. You will experience frustration that you aren't spending time with your buddies. You may blame marriage or career for taking something away from you, and this in turn will create distress that will negatively affect your marriage or career. By acknowledging the loss, you also take responsibility for your own choices; by grieving, you learn to let go of regret.

BE CAREFUL OF WHAT YOU WISH FOR

Let me introduce the next step by way of what I call the "dream house" analogy. Many people fantasize about one day constructing their perfect house, a house that generally requires more money than they currently have and is thus contingent on some future success. A typical couple might talk about their dream house constantly; they may even have an architect draw plans for it. Finally, the success they require comes and they are able to build the house. The months required to build it are fraught with excitement; it's exhilarating to watch it as it takes shape. The couple moves in, and those first few days are euphoric.

Then they begin to feel awful. Their negative feelings start with a nagging doubt: "Is this all there is?" They feel they're not as happy as they thought they would be. Then there is a sense of, "Do we deserve this?" Friends and family visit the dream house, and half of them never return. It may be that the visitors are jealous—the dream house couple has moved on with their life, and the visitors haven't, so there's a gap between them: "That's an awful lot of house for someone your age," they're told. A puzzling depression sets in. Though the depression doesn't lift, its intensity is diluted and translated into a cynical lethargy. When people visit, the owners no longer show it off proudly. Instead, they deemphasize its uniqueness and devalue its importance.

Now that you understand this "be careful what you wish for" syndrome, let's go on to the next step.

> *STEP 2: Envision obtaining something for which you've wished. It may be a promotion, a new job, a raise; or it can be something material, like a car or a boat. Pretend this wish has been granted, and then ask yourself: (a)How do you think people closest to you (personal or professional) would feel about you after you obtained your wish? (b)How would they act toward you? (c)Identify one positive reaction they might have and one negative reaction. (d)How would you feel about that negative reaction?*

It's possible that you would feel terrible about that negative reaction, in which case you could sabotage whatever fulfilled wish came your way. When you envision this scenario, however, and anticipate how you feel about a loss that the negative reaction might presage, you are much less likely to resort to sabotage. Instead, you can make a conscious choice about working through the loss rather than allowing your subconscious to be your guide.

ACKNOWLEDGING LOSS

The third and final step requires you to involve the people in key relationships in a discussion of how they feel about a loss. Too often, people ignore the loss or only discuss it in cognitive terms: "Since Company Y took us over and downsized, I have been doing twice the work." But how does this person and others in his or her group feel about the loss of the people they used to work with?

This third step uses a common relocation example. But if you find the example irrelevant to your circumstances, simply substitute any relevant situation in which a group loss has taken place.

> *STEP 3. A businessperson receives a sought-after promotion, and he and his family move across the country. The new job is great and the businessperson is doing well, but his family hates it. The kids miss their friends and his spouse misses the job she gave up when they relocated. The businessperson is also miserable because his family is so upset. But no one talks about their feelings, except in veiled references: "You look a little down in the dumps today, son," the father notes. "Anything wrong?" "No," the son replies, "no one at school was very friendly today."*
>
> *The exercise here is to round up family members on a Sunday afternoon, turn off the phones, and sit down and discuss what's missing in everyone's lives since they moved. It's a powerful experience for the kids to see one parent on the verge of tears saying how much she misses her old job, home, or neighborhood; or for the other spouse to say that he misses the people he used to work with and finds the new company highly impersonal. Most people in relationships have never "grieved" anything together. But doing so helps everyone talk about their feelings of loss regularly and within a common, realistic context. It's therapeutic to acknowledge and express feelings and identify the real issues. This way, people get unstuck and move on with their lives.*

How to grieve losses is a process that both individuals and organizations need to learn. The next chapter will help you work with that process and understand how organizational and individual success issues are inextricably linked.

CHAPTER

SUCCESS AND GROWTH AS A GRIEVING PROCESS

In the previous two chapters, we saw how success and change are accompanied by loss. Part of changing our attitude about change is learning to acknowledge and accept those losses. Managers cannot afford to ignore this reality or expect employees simply to "deal with it." Losses both tangible and intangible can lead to self-destructive behaviors that can ruin careers and damage companies.

These behaviors frequently seem inexplicable: The individual who receives a promotion becomes depressed, or the head of a growing company finds himself or herself unable to delegate. Not only can these behaviors be explained, however, but they can be understood as part of a natural and inevitable process: the grieving process. As Dr. Elizabeth Kübler-Ross explained years ago, this five-stage process enables people to come to terms with the loss of a loved one or with their own mortality. In this chapter, we're going to look at how this same five-stage process can help people deal with losses that come with change, growth, and success.

Because most businesspeople don't associate this grieving process with their behavior in a work environment, I'd like to clarify a few critical points about it.

First, each stage of the process—shock and denial, anger, bargaining, depression, and acceptance—is functional.

When I tell my audiences about the grieving process, their first reaction is, "Is there any way to get around these stages? We have a business to run, and we don't want our people spending their time being angry or depressed."

Unfortunately, there is no way around any stage. If you attempt to hurry people through this process and they skip a stage, they will be unproductive for a more sustained period than if they had worked through each stage. For instance, a CEO may seem to be dealing well with the changes caused by the growth of his company. After some initial denial, he skips anger and goes straight to bargaining; he is unwilling to let the anger surface, keeping a tight rein on that emotion. But sooner or later, that anger will emerge. Perhaps he becomes a holy terror months later and is impossible to deal with. No one in the office can figure out what has gotten into him, but no one wants to go near him. His anger is out of sequence. When it is out of sequence, a functional stage spawns dysfunctional behavior.

Second, when people go through the process in a healthy manner, they'll recycle through it in a diluted fashion.

In other words, once is not enough. People should go through the five stages as many times as necessary. Each time they go through, however, the intensity of emotion will be diminished. For instance, the first time an employee hears that the company is being sold, she may be so furious she wants to quit. When she recycles through a little later, her anger translates into, "I'm not happy with this change, but I guess management had no choice." The third time, her anger manifests itself in this lukewarm reaction: "Maybe it's for the best in the long run."

Third, the initial response to a loss should be strong and dramatic; acute grief is productive but chronic grief is not.

The initial emotions at each stage of the process should be intense. People who shrug off a loss are inviting chronic grief. They're the ones who whine about the same thing for years; who regularly complain that since the company's ownership changed ten years ago, the work environment has never been the same. Instead of expressing their feelings when the ownership change occurred, they allow grief to seep out slowly as bitterness and cynicism. As a result, they're stuck in the past. Their chronic grief condemns them to live in the past, like an endlessly grieving widow whose life ended for all practical purposes when her husband died, even though she outlived him by twenty years.

The grieving process can be managed and facilitated. You can help yourself and your people get through it and emerge stronger and more productive. To do so, you need to understand the specific function of each stage, the point at which people get unproductively stuck and how to get them unstuck.

STAGE ONE: SHOCK AND DENIAL

The function of this first stage is to buffer our realization of how much we've lost so it doesn't hit us full force. If we were to absorb the blow of the loss immediately, we'd become vegetables—we wouldn't be able to handle it. I used to consult with police officers who had to deliver the news of a loved one's death to a family. I told them that when they knocked at the door at four in the morning and informed the family of the death, they should expect and be reassured by the response they usually received: "Oh no, it can't be true, there must be some mistake." That denial is a healthy, functional response. If, on the other hand, family members were to respond in a cool, calm, and collected fashion, seemingly dealing with the news well, they would have skipped to the fifth stage, acceptance, and will pay for it later.

In a business environment, management often encourages this acceptance at the expense of the complete process. When a company is purchased, managers dread hearing their people say, "Oh, this is terrible, it can't be possible that we were acquired after all these years." Yet for employees to smile and say, "Oh, they're a good company, I'm sure everything will be fine" is unrealistically accepting a loss that should be unacceptable at first. Management needs to recognize these types of statements for what they really are: forms of denial. It's a mistake to assume people have adapted to a loss when all they've done is deny it.

On the other hand, it's just as deleterious to an organization for its people to become stuck in shock and denial. But all too often, they do get stuck in one of the following four ways:

- Inability to delegate

- Inability to take ownership of one's achievements

- Resistance to being the boss

- Minimization of wealth and possessions

INABILITY TO DELEGATE

Delegation is de facto recognition that a loss has occurred and that things have changed. But many of us prefer to deny that things have changed, and then we're stuck. If we do everything ourselves, then we avoid confronting the fact that we have to give something up—first and foremost of which is control. When people are promoted, for example, they often continue to do all the tasks they've always done even though they now have subordinates to do them. Companies encourage this mindset when they promote individuals to management roles and enthuse, "It's an opportunity of a lifetime." But they never encourage discussions of what these people will give up—what they'll have to delegate—when they step into managerial jobs.

INABILITY TO TAKE OWNERSHIP OF ONE'S ACHIEVEMENTS

You're stuck in denial when you regularly downplay kudos and compliments. Abnegating your success represents more than humility. When we succeed through hard work and skill and then blatantly lie to others about why we succeeded, we're in the rut of denial. Some responses to compliments that clearly indicate a successful individual is in this rut include

"I just lucked out."

"It was nothing."

"I was in the right place at the right time."

"It really was (another person or people) who did it."

RESISTANCE TO BEING THE BOSS

People stuck in denial are unable to assert their legitimate authority over subordinates. The classic example is the fast-track boss who can't bring herself to ask her secretary to type a memo or who can only beg and plead, as if she were asking him to do her a great favor. Individuals in this denial trap haven't differentiated between personal and professional parity. Professional parity is impossible in any growing organization—unless there is a hierarchy of authority and risk, nothing will get done and no one will grow and develop. The manager who pleads with his subordinate to do something, however, finds it difficult to assert that authority. He worries that if he does assert authority, he is somehow saying to that subordinate, "I'm better than you are." But he's saying nothing of the kind. What he is saying is that "given my higher level of risk, I have prerogatives you don't have." Personal parity, however, can and should exist between boss and subordinate, even when the former tells the latter what to do—the boss has no more personal validity than the subordinate.

MINIMIZATION OF WEALTH AND POSSESSIONS

People stuck in this first stage make concerted efforts to hide or downplay material symbols of their success. They're also uncomfortable with spending significant amounts of money on themselves. A perfect example is a former client of mine, the owner of a highly successful company who made over $10 million annually. We had numerous conversations in which he'd agonize over whether he should buy the cheapest Mercedes; he could afford to buy ten of the most expensive cars Mercedes sold without making a dent in his bank account.

People stuck here are denying their responsibility for their wealth and success as well as the distance from their roots that taking ownership would create. Our society has stereotyped high achievers as at best a different species and at worst as ruthless men and women who step on and over people in their rush to the top. As a result, many successful people shrink from their success, convinced that it will isolate them or create a picture of them as ethically tainted.

HOW TO GET UNSTUCK FROM DENIAL

No matter how people are stuck, the way to extricate them (or yourself) is by pushing them toward the next stage, which in this case is anger. This type of pushing is typically frowned on by management. We don't like our people to get upset and angry; we irrationally equate an angry employee with an unproductive, disruptive one.

Moving people from stage one to stage two can be accomplished by bringing submerged anger to the surface. Let's say a company has recently completed a merger, resulting in many changes. One executive, however, seems unable to delegate anything in the wake of the merger. She may well admit that this is a problem, but she'll insist that it's a minor one she'll deal with. Her boss might then say, "This company is quite different from what it was before; how do you feel about that?" The employee will answer, "It's fine with me." The boss can then say, "If my life had changed the way yours had, I'd be really mad. I don't believe for a second everything is fine. Isn't there anything that upsets you since the company merged?" "Well," the employee starts, "I guess I'm pretty ticked off about the way the new bonus system works."

As this employee becomes worked up, the denial is worked out and she is ready to move to the next stage.

STAGE TWO: ANGER

The function of anger is to place blame. We can't fully let go of a loss until we fully identify the culprit. Whether or not a real culprit exists is irrelevant. The feelings attached to the need must be expressed (to place blame) if we are to move on with our lives. When someone loses his spouse, he naturally wants to blame someone. The anger is at the spouse for leaving him. Because the spouse isn't there to get angry at, the anger emerges and blame is placed on others— doctors are a convenient target. Similarly, we become angry at owners who sell our company, or at our headhunter who encouraged us to take a new position. We are compelled to become angry and place blame—who isn't angry when he loses something he cares about?

As therapeutic as this stage is, it is also one where people frequently become stuck. Here are three common ways in which they become bogged down in anger:

- Constant, unrelenting criticism and pickiness
- Impossible-to-achieve standards and expectations
- A sense of superiority and arrogance

CONSTANT, UNRELENTING CRITICISM AND PICKINESS

People are often enraged about losses that occur in growing organizations—they miss the old traditions and camaraderie and would love to blame someone for the shifts that have occurred. But rather than confront the painful and real issues that come with growth, people who get stuck become nitpickers and critics. Their unexpressed anger has to come out in some fashion, and it frequently emerges as a barrage of trivial, critical remarks that make no sense to others.

IMPOSSIBLE-TO-ACHIEVE STANDARDS AND EXPECTATIONS

When people haven't dealt with their anger over a loss, they will be dissatisfied no matter what you do. They're the group heads who set unrealistic quarterly objectives. They're the ones who receive a wonderful promotion, beautiful new office, and a great raise, yet they believe it's not sufficient. Individuals as well as the organization can never live up to their standards. These are examples of "crooked" anger—instead of expressing their anger straightforwardly and directly, they do so indirectly.

A SENSE OF SUPERIORITY AND ARROGANCE

Who are the most arrogant and superior people you deal with? Often the most visibly successful. Because they haven't dealt with the losses caused by their success—or their underlying fear of not being able to maintain their success—they use arrogance and superiority to create distance and ward off invisible challengers. I'm not talking about people who are genuinely confident or individuals who occasionally flash an arrogant smile or strike a superior pose. People who are stuck in anger march around the office for months as if they're lords of the castle.

HOW TO GET UNSTUCK FROM ANGER

To move people out of anger into the next stage, get them to express disappointment. I've found that the following questions often catalyze an expression of disappointment:

- What are we missing now that we had before?

- What would you like to be here that isn't here now?

- How would you like the company to be?

The point of these questions isn't to promise that things will be the way they were, but to help people realize how disappointed they are about the things they've lost. Management usually makes a mistake with people stuck in anger. Rather than encouraging them to express their disappointment, they try to convince them that their new situation is far better than before and shouldn't be experienced as disappointing. The following example, though not an illustration of an earthshaking loss, should be familiar to everyone: The efficiency of voice mail is great, but its widespread use also causes us to lose a certain type of human interaction. We feel genuine disappointment over this loss. That doesn't mean that we get rid of voice mail; it does mean we need to acknowledge and articulate our disappointment.

STAGE THREE: BARGAINING

The purpose of bargaining is to cut one's losses. In this stage, people who have experienced success no longer want any more, because they associate success with loss. The company has expanded, a new strategy has been launched, new management has been brought in— whatever the form of success, it has exacted too great a price and people want it to stop (subconsciously, of course). The bargain they strike is this: If I don't achieve anything else, then I don't have to lose any more. People most often become stuck in this stage when they avoid challenge in their personal and work relationships. The two ways people get stuck are

- Creating unequal relationships

- Sustaining unchallenging friendships

CREATING UNEQUAL RELATIONSHIPS

Highly successful men and women often choose spouses who are clearly less successful and less growth oriented. Men marry bimbos, women marry deadbeats, and everyone wonders how in the world these hard-charging high achievers could find spouses who are so obviously wrong for them. The unconscious bargain these successful people make is, "I've driven myself to be successful and I've accomplished a great deal, but it has cost me, and enough is enough. I intend to have a calm, nondisruptive personal life, and that means finding a spouse who won't challenge me." Consciously, of course, people rationalize their choice of mates by saying, "Oh, she really gets along with people well" or "He's really a nice guy and great with kids."

This scenario has become an especially acute problem for women. Raised in a culture in which they were taught to be caretakers, businesswomen frequently find mates who need mothers, and the marriage becomes more of a child/parent relationship than husband/wife. Although the women's movement may have helped women become successful professionals, it hasn't prevented them from carrying on their traditional caretaking role. It is almost as if being a successful professional isn't enough; being a caretaker of someone else is still equated with complete fulfillment.

Men not only choose unequal spouses, but they often have affairs because of this choice. Contrary to what many people believe, highly successful men don't have affairs for sex and physical attractiveness—their wives are frequently more attractive than their mistresses. They have affairs because they're searching for someone to talk to—they certainly can't talk to their complacent, unchallenging spouses.

Rather than searching for unequal partners, some people create them. They choose equally bright, growth-oriented people for mates and then push them into becoming bimbos and deadbeats. They strike their bargains after the fact rather than before. They literally stupefy their partners with their partner's usually unconscious cooperation.

Unequal personal relationships have a professional fallout. No one can set ambitious professional goals and plan to establish challenging, productive business relationships if the most important relationship in their personal life is unequal. As I've stated before, professional relationships mirror personal ones. In this situation, the blended life of our new paradigm becomes impossible.

SUSTAINING UNCHALLENGING FRIENDSHIPS

This is similar to the previous manifestation, except that business-people remain friends with people they outgrew years ago. One of the most common examples is the CEO who regularly attends get-togethers with his college fraternity buddies. He's grown enormously in the years since graduation, yet his buddies still retain the same frat-house mentality. Why does he continue to maintain these and similar friendships? Because they don't challenge him. Hard-driving business colleagues or members of a professional organization wouldn't allow him to coast. You can see this phenomenon in managers who keep buddies in roles where they're no longer productive and don't confront issues. In this instance, bargaining involves the exchange of production for friendliness.

HOW TO GET UNSTUCK FROM BARGAINING

Being stuck in unequal relationships manifests itself in other ways at work. People who compromise with relationships also compromise with the change going on around them at work. They are willing to accept a little change, but no more. They will make a few changes, but that's where they draw the line—they are compelled to limit the losses.

To help people move through this bargaining stage, you need to get them to understand and accept the full ramifications of change. For instance, a manager has installed a new technology for his department. But he has closed his eyes to what this new technology means; that he'll have to replace a number of people in his department, that he'll need to change his policies and procedures to accommodate this technology, and on and on.

To help unstick people's attitudes about change, ask the following questions:

- What does a specific change or changes in the organization mean in terms of your area?

- What does it mean in terms of people—hiring, firing, skills required, and so on?

- What does it mean in terms of work behaviors?

- How long will the change last?

The last question is often the clincher. Many people think change is short term—in six weeks, this will all be over. When you help them realize that the change is ongoing and will require years rather than months, the full impact hits them. That impact won't make them happy, but that's fine because it moves them to the next stage.

STAGE FOUR: DEPRESSION

The function of depression is to integrate change fully. In most organizations, however, depression is viewed as dysfunctional. Management often assumes that it isn't good for the organization ever to have unhappy employees—low morale for any reason has taken on almost sinister connotations in many companies. As a result, management turns itself into walking, talking smile buttons, trying to cheer everyone up. Managers tell everyone, "The merger is going to be great, you'll see." They insist that the downsizing will be beneficial. They tell people to look on the bright side of the massive restructuring. They accentuate only the positive points of the new culture. What management doesn't understand is that when people are depressed, they're at the threshold of acceptance.

When people become stuck in depression, they manifest the following three attitudes or behaviors:

- A movement toward isolation

- A sense of meaninglessness

- A lack of interest in or commitment to work

ISOLATION OF SUCCESS

When people aren't allowed to feel awful and work through their depression, they often retreat both literally and figuratively. As you ask this isolated person a question as he moves through the corridor, he responds, "I'll talk to you later." He stops dealing with issues and hides out in his office. He becomes one of the voice mail people. Success freaks people out. Unwilling to deal with the losses that come with success, they remove themselves from the daily reminders of what they've lost.

A SENSE OF MEANINGLESSNESS

Here is the thought that best characterizes this existential bog: "Is this all there is?" People often say that they've worked hard all their lives to reach goals, but when they reach them, they feel empty. This is a natural and inevitable feeling and part of a predictable process. It's depressing to realize that achieving a major goal isn't unalloyed joy; that there is a sad side to it. With the ability and permission to experience these sad feelings, we are able to appreciate fully our achievements and attained goals.

LACK OF INTEREST IN OR COMMITMENT TO WORK

People stuck in depression often begin to doubt that they're in the right jobs, careers, or organizations. Though they're successful, they're not happy. They question whether they were really cut out to be an attorney, a businessperson, or an accountant. Owners of companies sell what they've worked all their lives for in a fit of depression. Many times, these people switch careers or go back to school, convinced that these radical moves will be panaceas. Instead of dealing with their depression, they make inappropriate and counterproductive career and business decisions.

HOW TO GET UNSTUCK FROM DEPRESSION

The irony of unsticking yourself from depression is that you need to get the bleakest scenario possible out in the open. A group of employees faces major changes because they're embarking on a TQM program. After the CEO details the changes for them, he adds that there's no guarantee that the program will work, and the company may junk TQM and return to the old system if it doesn't pan out. That possibility is depressing. Although you would think that informing people of the worst possible scenario would make them feel worse, it actually lifts their spirits. People are relieved when the unstated is finally stated; they begin to come to terms with negative possibilities as soon as they're articulated. Studies of terminally ill people show that when doctors talk to them about their deaths, their condition often improves and they experience some relief. The point is that the way through and out of depression is to verbalize the doomsday scenario and surface all the unsurfaced fears.

STAGE FIVE: ACCEPTANCE

This stage isn't what it's cracked up to be. It is not picking the choice without a downside. We often believe that once we've accepted something—a new position, a new owner, a new strategy— everything will be fine.

In fact, loss comes with all choices, and the function of acceptance is to make a choice with a downside that you're willing to integrate into your life. For example, your company is bought. You have the choice of adapting to the new culture or taking early retirement and using the money to start your own business. With the first choice, you will definitely lose the old culture. With the second choice, you may lose significant amounts of money.

But there is no third choice that allows you to maintain the old culture, start your own business, and risk nothing. There is no choice that is all upside and no downside.

The following two characteristics signify true acceptance:

- A sense of one's limits
- A comfort with responsibility, power and authority.

A SENSE OF ONE'S LIMITS

Successful people who make it all the way through to this stage of the grieving process say, "This is what I do well, this is what I don't do well, and I accept those limits." They don't try to be all things to all people; they don't equate success with caretaking. They're willing to accept the losses they've sustained—they can delegate the tasks they used to do routinely, and they are willing to leave old relationships behind.

A FEELING OF COMFORT
WITH RESPONSIBILITY, POWER, AND AUTHORITY

Rather than apologizing for their position and power, these people accept it unilaterally. They also distinguish between personal and professional parity; they accept the organizational hierarchy and how it creates unequal professional relationships, and they also realize that personal relationships remain equal.

HOW TO KEEP RECYCLING

Acceptance isn't an endpoint; it's simply the starting point for the next cycle through the grieving process. If you believe that your acceptance entitles you to a free ride for the next ten years, you're in for a rude awakening. Other changes and losses are just around the bend. When they occur, recognize that you'll start back in denial and have to work your way through the five stages again.

WHY NOW?

People have always gone through the grieving process. It's intuitive, and people naturally go through the five stages described. But it doesn't have to be an unacknowledged process. By acknowledging and articulating what is involved, you facilitate people's movement through it.

Such facilitation is necessary in a high risk culture. In the past, high-profit organizations could hide or transfer the dysfunctional people who became stuck at some stage. We were able to give people more time to struggle through the depression or anger that often made them unproductive or difficult to deal with.

In a high risk culture, however, successful people in growing organizations need to learn to move through the process as quickly and efficiently as possible and help others do the same. Doing this will truly change our attitude toward change.

PART THREE
OVERCOMING
COMMON
OBSTACLES

CHAPTER

CLARIFYING
CONFUSED
VALUES

Now that we've examined the murky complexities of the success and growth process, we will look at the force that can clarify this process and give meaningful direction to our lives: values.

The last paradigm discussed in Chapter 2 dealt with values: We should create value-driven personal and professional lives. And in Chapter 4 (see page 55) we saw that values determine our priorities, which in turn direct the decision-making process. You can think of values as the basic apparatus you are using to keep you in motion as you work without a net. Unless you understand this apparatus— your values—you won't maximize your success, and you may even sabotage it.

THE VALUE
CLARIFICATION INSTRUMENT

At the beginning of this book, I asked you to complete a value clarification exercise (page 10) and save your responses for later. The core value indicators around which the exercise revolved—responsibility, change and reward/payoff—are the key values that matter in a high risk culture. All the things that we usually think about when we consider values—honesty, hard work, compassion, loyalty—are subsumed by these three core value indicators.

This instrument will also help you in a number of other ways. Three of the most common ways businesspeople use it are for:

- Recruitment and selection

- Getting the management team unstuck

- Retention and promotion of individuals within an organization

We'll discuss these uses of the instrument later in this chapter. First, however, we'll look at the implications of each of the ten types of statements.

1A. A job is a privilege extended to an employee by an employer.

1B. A job is an inherent right guaranteed by society.

1C. I feel equally divided between response A and response B.

This first item measures *accountability*, and statement A is the high risk response. When given an ultimatum that a task must be done properly or else, high risk people say, "Tell me what to do, and I'll either do it or quit." Their response is unequivocal, and they don't question the employer's right to tell them what to do.

Statement B, on the other hand, is a low risk response and will lead to the perception that a demand for performance is an intolerable ultimatum. Low risk people question a company's right to hold them accountable. They're the ones who, when you give them a job to do and they don't do it properly, complain that it wasn't their fault and that someone else was responsible. To them, a job is what society owes them.

2A. People begin to change when they feel comfortable, supported, and positively reinforced.

2B. People begin to change when they become more uncomfortable than comfortable with their current circumstances.

2C. I feel equally divided between response A and response B.

This item raises the question of why people *begin* to change. The italicized word is important, because I'm not referring to why people continue to change, a different matter entirely. The low risk response

(A) theorizes that people change when they're comfortable. As a result, low risk managers fall into the trap of bribing people to change: "If you'll agree to the transfer, we'll increase your salary." This managerial extortion bankrupts companies morally and financially.

This isn't to say that all incentives are counterproductive. They're useful as motivators when people are already in a change mode. But incentives don't initiate change.

The high risk response, that injecting discomfort into relationships initiates change, becomes self-evident when we ask ourselves a simple question: Has anyone ever made significant changes in their lives because everything was going well?

3A. Security is best defined through tangible things—living in one place for an extended period of time, job security, having the same friends.

3B. Security is best defined though factors that are primarily internal—certainty about your marketability in different settings and jobs, the knowledge that you can meet your personal and professional needs.

3C. I feel equally divided between response A and response B.

The issue here is really *flexibility and adaptability* (or lack thereof), not security. Low risk statement A means that the person who defines security as relating to external factors—home, geography, steady job—will view any change in those areas as intolerable and be highly inflexible. The low risk person will wait forever for the steel industry to be reborn in his town; he'll refuse to accept the fact that it's not coming back and that he'll have to move to find a new job.

The high risk statement (B) indicates that security is based on internal factors—by one's marketability (for any relevant job in any organization) and one's portability (you take your marketability with you wherever you go). These people are highly flexible and adaptable, because their sense of security isn't dependent on a particular place or person.

4A. Failure is as important to the learning process as success; try and minimize failure and you decrease your capacity to learn.

4B. People learn best through successful experiences; try and maximize success and eliminate failure.

4C. I feel equally divided between response A and response B.

This is another change-related item. The low risk response (B) means that we're so afraid of failure that we'll do anything to avoid that possibility; that we won't take chances or learn new things because we might screw up and fail. Stagnation and plateauing are common in people who view failure as a dirty word. Given an exciting opportunity to learn a new skill, low risk people turn down the opportunity because the learning process would place them in unfamiliar territory where doing poorly is much more likely than in their safe, familiar jobs.

The high risk response (A) means tolerating failure. High risk people view failure as simply another learning experience. It does not mean that they encourage it or reward multiple mistakes—people who don't learn from initial failure are either brain damaged or passive-aggressive.

How you respond to your subordinates' initial failures will have a tremendous impact on whether they adopt a high risk or low risk posture. If you respond to a mistake by screaming at them, calling them names, and refusing to discuss what went wrong, they'll devote all their energy to covering their mistakes and avoiding any projects that aren't sure things. If, however, you respond by helping your people analyze and learn from their mistakes, they will grow and develop (and be willing to risk making mistakes now and again).

Anyone who is failure-averse should remember that highly successful people all admit they've failed at something, and mediocre performers insist they're perfect.

  5A. Homelessness and other related problems are social problems; they reflect society's inability to deal effectively with social issues.

  5B. With the exception of a small number of defined populations, homelessness and other related problems are not social problems; they are expressions of individual choice.

  5C. I feel equally divided between response A and response B.

Here we return to the responsibility issue. Who is responsible for what happens to us: external forces or ourselves? The high risk position is B—ourselves. The low risk position is that people are in certain negative situations not because of their choices but because of forces beyond their control.

This item often raises people's hackles; they criticize the high risk stance as a particularly brutal form of social Darwinism. No one chooses to be fired or to grow up in an urban ghetto, they maintain. Though it's true that we don't always make the choices that place us in difficult situations, it's also true that we have choices about our response to those situations. For instance, there are two responses to unemployment: I better get moving and acquire new skills to get another job because this industry is kaput. Or, there's not much I can do because there aren't any jobs in this town and in this industry, so I better just sit tight until things get better.

Low risk people will face increasing unemployment in high-change cultures. They want others to initiate and take responsibility for their adaptation to change and new demands.

6A. Confrontation and conflict are two types of problem-solving strategies—everyone can use them effectively.

6B. Confrontation and conflict are last-resort strategies, and they often make matters worse.

6C. I feel equally divided between response A and response B.

Do you believe people are resilient or fragile? If resilient, you chose the high risk A; if fragile, you picked the low risk B. People only engage in conflict to the degree that they believe others are resilient. If they believe they're fragile, they'll avoid anything that would push the other person over the edge.

Your choice here not only indicates how you feel about the fragility/resilience of others, but how you feel about yourself. If you avoid confronting people because you think they'll fall apart, you're really worried that you would fall apart.

High risk people believe that they and others possess self-protective mechanisms that enable them to survive any conflict or confrontation. This is true in even the worst-case scenarios. An employee had a nervous breakdown last year, and now you have to give him a negative performance review. The high risk position is that this employee is capable of handling the bad news; he may handle it by denying (to himself) everything you tell him. Or he may have another nervous breakdown. But if he does, the high risk position is that he exercised the choice, and that it is presumptuous for any individual to assume that he or she has sufficient power over another human being to be the main cause of such a disturbing event.

7A. An employee's personal problems are none of an employer's business as long as the employee is doing his or her job adequately.

7B. Sooner or later, personal problems aggravate work problems, and vice versa. Employers have an obligation to employees to hold them accountable for developing plans designed to resolve personal problems that affect work performance.

7C. I feel equally divided between response A and response B.

The low risk perspective (A) is that if you do an adequate job at work, the company shouldn't be concerned about anything else. Why should an organization care if John has a mistress or Mary has a gambling problem, as long as they meet the requirements of their jobs?

On the surface, this accountability issue is the source of much controversy and debate. But if you probe beneath the surface of most organizations, you'll find a link between employees' personal behavior and how organizations treat them. For instance, people get fired all the time for who they are rather than what they've done (or have not done) on the job. Companies may find narrowly work-related rationales to justify the firings, but the real reasons are that they're alcoholics who refuse to deal with their drinking or they have some other problems they won't address.

The high risk perspective isn't based on some ethical or moral construct. Instead, it presumes that how one behaves personally mirrors how one will behave professionally. As one person I know put it when referring to a particular executive who was notoriously unfaithful to his wife, "If he'll screw anything that walks, why don't you think he'll screw the company?" There are no business problems—only business manifestations of personal problems.

This perspective doesn't mean you must become a moral purist, firing someone because she drives over the speed limit or fails to go to church each Sunday. What it does mean is that you must decide on your particular set of values. There should be a match between your values and those of your organization and the people with whom you work and associate.

8A .Both money earned and impact created in one's job are necessary measures of success in one's work.

8B. Either money earned or impact created in one's job is a valid measure of success in one's work.

8C. I feel equally divided between response A and response B.

This is the only item that focuses on the reward/payoff value, and the statements reveal why we work. Statement A is the high risk response because it takes the uncompromising position that we have two drives in our work: money and impact. The low risk alternative (B) is a compromise between money and impact.

The drive for money is actually the drive to create choices in our lives. In a society where both rich and poor possess credit cards, we no longer work primarily so we can buy "things." The difference between rich and poor people is that the former have more options. Rich people have the option to live in nicer neighborhoods than poor people, for instance.

The drive for impact means intentionally changing people as a result of your interaction with them. For instance, a financial planner changes people in the sense that he helps them achieve educational, lifestyle, and retirement goals that they couldn't achieve without his assistance. Another example: the founder of a company called Creative Playthings started her business because she was fed up with toys that only entertained; she wanted toys that also taught children something about the world. These people change those around them because of what they do, and at the same time they make money.

The high risk ideal is a 50/50 split between money and impact. People who only want to have an impact are closet public servants. In a for-profit organization, they will plateau and will cease to be productive; they don't need to create any more options in their life and most likely will have little or no growth drive. On the other hand, people who only work for money might as well go into organized crime—they're the ones who cause problems in companies because of dishonesty or lack of commitment.

Our society, however, fosters the myth that we must choose between money and impact: We can be social workers or teachers and have impact, but we have to forsake money. Or the opposite but equally common notion perpetuated by society is that we can make tons of money, but we won't have the satisfaction of doing something meaningful.

Although it's true that some professions like teaching don't provide significant financial rewards (because of low risk traditions such as tenure), the vast majority of people can embrace both the drive for money and the drive for impact.

9A. The best personal relationships are based on common interests, activities, and backgrounds.

9B. The best personal relationships are based on each person's demand for personal growth from oneself and the other person.

9C. I feel equally divided between response A and response B.

This item is similar to item 2, in which we measured comfort versus discomfort within the context of the change value. Here we're looking at what catalyzes growth and change in relationships. The low risk answer is A—commonalities. The high risk answer is B—challenge. High risk people stay together and grow because they challenge each other and inject discomfort into the relationship. Low risk people may stay together for years, but they may also hate each other, hiding beneath the false reassurance of common interests and no arguments.

10A. Many people have two or three strikes against them from the start and often end up as victims through no fault of their own.

10B. With the exception of physical or mental handicaps, adults are never victims; they create their own problems and can create their own solutions.

10C. I feel equally divided between response A and response B.

This is similar to the responsibility value of item 5. Here, the low risk statement is A, and the high risk one is B. Contrary to what you might think, the high risk posture is not cold-hearted and elitist. In fact, this posture is highly optimistic about what people can accomplish, whereas the low risk statement is very pessimistic. Though it's true that rising from difficult circumstances and situations is hard, it's by no means impossible. We all can exercise choices that enable us to avoid victimization. Rather than adopting a paternalistic, caretaking attitude in response to those less fortunate than ourselves, high risk people believe that everyone has the capacity to grow and succeed.

EVALUATING THE PROFILE

You should now have a sense of the implications of your responses (or those of subordinates) to each of the ten items. But it's also important to get a sense of what the sum of your responses implies. Specifically, is your profile high risk, low risk, or value confused?

Begin by charting your responses to each item on the answer sheet. Then see how they compare to the three "pure" profiles shown here.

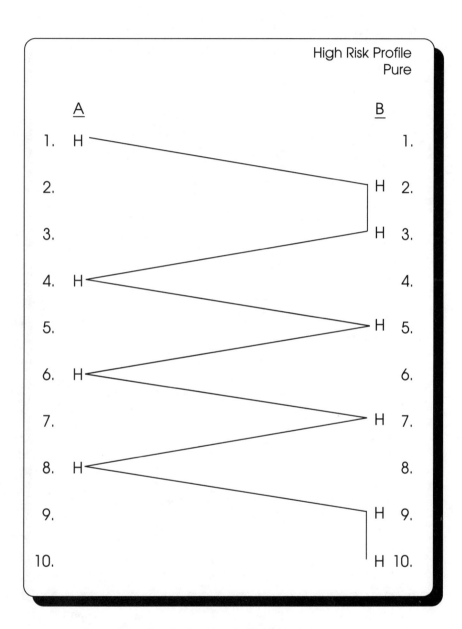

VALUE CLARIFICATION INSTRUMENT

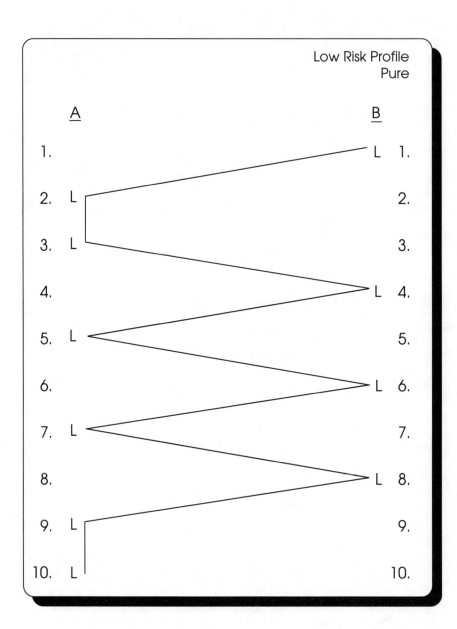

VALUE CLARIFICATION INSTRUMENT *(CONTINUED)*

	Value Confused Profile Pure	
<u>A</u>	<u>C</u>	<u>B</u>
1.	H/L	
2.	H/L	
3.	H/L	
4.	H/L	
5.	H/L	
6.	H/L	
7.	H/L	
8.	H/L	
9.	H/L	
10.	H/L	

VALUE CLARIFICATION INSTRUMENT *(CONTINUED)*

It's important to understand the connotations of the profile that most clearly resembles your own. The following will give you a sense of what those connotations are:

- **High risk profile.** In the areas where you're high risk, you'll be clearest in setting expectations of others and have the greatest chance of those expectations being met. Although you'll receive the clearest results in high risk areas, you'll also be managing a high degree of conflict.

- **Low risk profile.** In low risk areas, you're unclear in setting expectations and least likely to get them met. Although you won't have to manage much conflict, you're consensus driven and generally get poor results.

- **Value confused profile.** You're sending out the greatest number of mixed messages, and a high degree of confusion surrounds you. You're trying to be all things to all people.

Let me add a few comments about the value-confused profile. First, most people who complete this value clarification instrument have a few C responses. The problem comes when people have six or more value-confused responses. That's when they're likely to become dysfunctional and ill more than other people. Stress research shows that trying to be all things to all people is unhealthy. At the same time, however, our culture has pushed us in this direction, sending the message that success comes to those who make everyone happy. In fact, the most successful people are those who take clear, unambiguous positions—positions that can cause others to be quite unhappy.

Not only can you use this value clarification instrument to locate your profile, but you can use it to spotlight and address specific value problems. For instance, Jack is a very bright and talented lower-grade manager. Though he possesses a number of good skills, he hasn't received a promotion in years. Jack completed the value clarification instrument, and we saw that a large number of responses were high risk; number 6, however, was low risk. As his response indicated, Jack avoided conflict and confrontation. After we talked with Jack, we learned that he thought people were very fragile and therefore never placed demands on them. It quickly became clear to Jack that unless he learned how to confront people, he'd never help them (or himself) develop the decision-making and relationship-building skills required in a growth-oriented, high risk organization. Without those skills, Jack (and those individuals in his department) suffered from blocked productivity and would never be considered for promotion.

HOW TO MOVE TOWARD HIGH RISK POSITIONS

For Jack or anyone else who finds a value clarification response that is confused or low risk, the objective is to move oneself toward the high risk end of the continuum. The best way to do this is by starting to take little risks in a given area. For instance, Jack might start by confronting people on minor issues. Then, when he realizes that the confrontations hurt neither himself nor others, he can take on larger issues.

Every time people take a risk and survive, they develop a greater tolerance for risk. By gradually escalating your level of risk, you move yourself slowly but surely toward a high risk position.

ORGANIZATIONAL USES OF THE INSTRUMENT

As I noted early in this chapter, value clarification isn't just for individuals. Organizations can use this tool in the following three ways:

- Recruitment/selection

- Unstalling the management team

- Retention/promotion

RECRUITMENT/SELECTION

The hiring process has become more difficult than ever before. Legal restrictions prevent interviewers from asking a number of key questions. In addition, prospective employees have read all the articles and books about what to say during job interviews, and placement services frequently coach them about how to present themselves.

Many human resource managers say that they don't know any more about a job candidate after the interview than they did before.

The value clarification instrument helps organizations dig below the surface of job applicants. It generates more in-depth information than most any other tool, and it does so in a way that stays within current legal guidelines. Most importantly, it helps organizations identify and hire individuals with high risk profiles—the people who have the highest growth and development potential and will contribute the most to organizations.

UNSTALLING THE MANAGEMENT TEAM

Many management teams engage in seemingly unresolvable conflicts and in lengthy, frustrating, and unproductive meetings. When everyone on the management team completes this instrument, we often find that people are not at loggerheads over content but over values. When there are people with diametrically opposed values on the same team, they will never work well together. Value clarification allows the team to see where the real conflicts are; it enables the team to confront value differences and determine who's out of step with the company's values.

RETENTION/PROMOTION

The third use is the most obvious. It gives companies a tool to identify employees who are in or out of tune with organizational values. It provides an additional tool for helping managers determine who is worth investing resources in and who would be better off in an organization with different values.

ONE FINAL NOTE ABOUT SCORES

If you or your people score poorly on this instrument—if you seem to be value confused or low risk on most items—it doesn't mean that you should resign yourself to stagnation and mediocrity. Rather than being a final exam, this instrument is a spot quiz that helps you identify problems before they become fatal to your job, your career, or your company. As soon as you spot a problem, you can begin the process of risk escalation in the appropriate area to increase your risk tolerance. If you do so, when you retake the instrument at a later date you'll find that your location on the risk continuum will have moved closer to the pure high risk profile.

C H A P T E R

COPING
WITH
DELAYED
DEVELOPMENT

In the previous chapter, we saw that the best apparatus for working without a net is a value-based management system. Much of the rest of this book, in one way or another, deals with building and maintaining such a system. This chapter discusses one of the biggest obstacles to a value system a company faces: the prolonged adolescence of employees.

If all your employees were adults in the best psychological and emotional senses of the word, then implementing the value-based management system discussed in the previous chapter would be a snap. Unfortunately, many of them are still adolescents in mind, if not in body. They are far more concerned about whether they have dates for the weekend than about values. If they were to complete the value clarification instrument from the previous chapter, they would most likely receive a value-confused or low risk classification.

Organizations can effectively implement value-based management systems only after they've recognized the delayed development of their people and learned how to adjust their management style to dovetail with the three different stages of development. Before discussing what those stages are and what you can do, let's focus on why so many people's development has been delayed.

THE SECRET IMPACT OF TECHNOLOGY: PROLONGED ADOLESCENCE

It's easy to see how technological advances affect employment, lifestyle, and economics. But it's difficult to see the more subtle impact on human development: delaying the process of maturation.

Technology is a glutton for knowledge and education. If we don't keep up with technological changes, we'll be out of a job. The computer illustrates this point. The steady stream of new and improved computing methods forces people who otherwise would have plateaued years ago to remain in a learning mode. New technologies have created a cottage industry of seminars and conferences designed to keep people up to speed on the latest developments and applications.

As a result of the technology revolution, our culture has become obsessed with both continuing and higher education. Around the turn of the century, grade-school teachers were barely literate—they had the equivalent of today's third-grade education. By World War II, a high school diploma was the sign of an educated person. Now, 2.5 years of college is the norm. In some circles and industries, a master's degree or doctorate is considered essential.

Though our society considers formal education a good thing, it comes at the price of experience. Most of the members of our workforce—especially the younger members—have traded life experience for head knowledge. As a result, they delay experiencing things such as marriage, families, and jobs until much later than previous generations. This lack of experience translates into the following four problems:

- Lack of common sense

- Avoidance of decision making

- Poor people skills

- Unstable personal lives

LACK OF COMMON SENSE

Overeducated, underexperienced employees are very good literal, sequential thinkers; they can move from A to B to C to D. But when asked to move from A to D, they're lost. Unless steps B and C are spelled out, they flounder. Let's say you ask an employee to put together materials for a sales presentation. You tell him the base of information you need, the purpose of the presentation, and who the audience will be. What you get back from him is a jumble of data, thrown together seemingly at random to meet your literal request. Common sense would dictate that the presentation be attractive and that certain statistics should be included and highlighted given the presentation's purpose and audience.

Extensive formal education turns people into linear thinkers who are heavily dependent on authority. That's why many very bright, young employees need to be told every step before they take it. These employees view their managers as instructors in the worst sense of the word—tell us the assignment, how to do it, spoonfeed us information, require us to regurgitate it back, discourage intuition, and we'll get it done.

AVOIDANCE OF DECISION MAKING

Decision making skills atrophy when you're in an environment that buffers you from reality for extensive time periods. Most students don't have to deal with nasty landlords, child rearing, and working through a marriage. Some postpone many of life's gut-wrenching decisions until they're in their late twenties. The toughest decision they have had to make is which class to take. It's no wonder that when these bright students graduate to the world of work, they're stupefied by even the simplest of decisions. More than one neophyte worker has been paralyzed by a decision between the company's Health Maintenance Organization and Preferred Provider Organization health plans.

POOR PEOPLE SKILLS

The academic universe is sheltered and largely homogeneous. If students are getting their financial needs satisfied by their parents, they don't have to learn to deal with other people besides faculty members (who are relatively accommodating). Because they're operating in an environment in which only a few repeatable and meetable demands are placed on them (primarily for grades of at least C or B), they haven't stretched themselves in their relationships. On their first jobs, however, they're often confronted by inane or insane colleagues who make outrageous demands; or by off-the-wall customers threatening to kill them if the order is shipped late. These new employees don't have the faintest idea how to handle such people.

UNSTABLE PERSONAL LIVES

Delayed developers have made few, if any, real commitments. For many middle-class people, marriage and kids have been pushed back to thirty years of age or later. In addition, they haven't made a meaningful, mature commitment to any organization. To them, notions such as stability and commitment are off somewhere in the distant future. They intend to extend adolescence as long as they can. When they enter the workplace, they expect and sometimes dictate a school atmosphere. In many organizations, they treat the summer as a three-month vacation. Even though they're physically at work, their minds are elsewhere.

THE NEW DEVELOPMENTAL STAGES

What developmental stage are your employees in? Because the three stages (adolescence, young adult, adult) have been delayed, it's difficult to tell by their chronological ages. In fact, those ages are frequently misleading.

Adolescence used to take place roughly between ages twelve and nineteen. Now it generally occurs between ages twenty and thirty. Employees in this age range manifest classic adolescent traits: inability to concentrate, short attention span, and a focus on their bodies and emerging sexuality. To them, work is a necessary evil. The following story illustrates this attitude, and it's one most businesspeople have experienced.

I recently was in a hurry to catch a plane and was attempting to turn in my keys at a car rental counter. The young woman behind the counter was engaged in an animated conversation with an equally young man. It was obvious that she was far more interested in developing an amorous relationship with him than in conducting a business one with me. When I interrupted her conversation to say that I really had to catch a flight, she was startled. It was clear what her priorities were—business relationships will come and go, but personal ones are special.

Managers are terribly frustrated by adolescent employees. They hire people in their twenties and expect that they'll act and work like adults if given the proper training. In fact, though they may look like adults, they're emotionally and psychologically still in their teens.

The second developmental stage, *young adulthood*, has shifted from ages twenty to thirty to ages thirty to forty. During this stage, people are making commitments to families and other significant relationships—they're often getting married, having children, and beginning to establish roots. At this point in their development, people begin to grasp the significance of process: the realization that it's not just getting to a destination that counts, it's also important how you get there.

Until managers reach this stage, they will focus on getting things done at any cost. Ruthless managers who ignore process don't care that they've offended half their staff in getting a job done. They may make deals and meet deadlines, but they cause their subordinates to request transfers and their customers to search for new suppliers.

An understanding and appreciation of process comes to a great degree from parenting. Every parent has observed his child engaged in a process. For instance, the parent might tell a five-year-old to get out of a car, but the child will only get out after he's engaged in a ritualized routine: finishing playing with a toy, honking the horn, playing with a doll, climbing back and forth between the seats. For a child, there is a defined way of getting things done, and parents learn to respect this process.

Consciously or unconsciously, people in this stage also learn to respect process at work. They realize that learning takes place through this process, and if they disrupt it, they disrupt the learning. Until people reach this second stage, they will be Atilla the Hun managers who say to their people, "I don't care what you think or how you feel about it, just do it."

The third and final stage is *adulthood*. Instead of beginning after thirty, it now commences after forty. Integration of the personal and professional takes place, as well as the establishment of tangible commitments. In this stage, people focus on their life's mission (or purpose), and their blended professional and personal actions articulate that mission. They realize that life isn't just about obtaining a prestigious job or making a specific amount of money. They now choose professions or solidify commitments to companies based on who they are and how they will be able to affect other people's lives. What they do allows them to articulate who they are every day. This group should be the foundation on which a value-based management system is built.

Adults are an organization's most productive people. Unfortunately, they're also the people most vulnerable to layoffs, early retirement, and downsizing. Because of delayed development, adults often hit their peak of productivity when the company is ready to get rid of them. The practice of enforced retirement at age sixty-five is even more ludicrous now than it was in the past; employees in this culture can be operating at peak levels in their seventies and eighties. They're highly productive in this stage because they're working for themselves, not just for money. In fact, they usually have a highly sophisticated understanding of the importance of both impact and money. They're committed to goals that drive performance, and therefore they approach their jobs with great focus and intensity.

Now that you're familiar with what each stage entails, let's examine what organizations can do to create an effective approach for people going through each developmental stage.

HOW TO DEAL WITH ADOLESCENT WORKERS

Rather than bemoan the fact that half your people act like teenagers, you need to accept that unfortunate but unavoidable fact and learn to make the best of it. The good news is that adolescents can be highly productive with the right structure. Though you can't (and shouldn't try to) eliminate the rebellion and testing that comes with this stage, you can structure an environment of discipline and limits that enables adolescent employees to function well. The four unbreakable rules of this environment are as follows:

1. **No interaction can last more than ten minutes.** Five minutes is actually preferable. Attempt to engage an adolescent in a thirty-minute talk and you'll find that his eyes have glazed and his mind has wandered.

2. **Every interaction is limited to one item.** Adolescents are overwhelmed by multiple items. When you try to discuss their absenteeism, the problem with a coworker, and their budget projections, they'll be unable to concentrate on any item. Never go into meetings with a laundry list. Instead, determine what

the single most important issue is and focus on that to the exclusion of all else.

3. **No lectures and teaching about general principles.** Managers are fond of telling their young subordinates, "This is what we do in this company, and it's up to you to figure out how you can fit in." Vague statements about how we're a company that believes in empowerment will go right over adolescents' heads. The key is to be specific and state what you want them to do in action terms.

4. **Ruthless consistency in rewarding positive behavior and punishing negative behavior**. This means not allowing one employee to arrive late because she lives far away or because she has to drop off her kids at school. Credibility is lost when managers are inconsistent in their rewards or punishments. Although adolescents will test their supervisors constantly—they'll scream and moan to their faces and behind their backs—they need them to meet every test with consistency.

When dealing with adolescent workers, don't forget that the goal is to see them through this stage and on to the next one. It may be tempting to fall back into a caretaking mode, but this is the last thing any employer should do. Follow the four unbreakable rules and adhere to the caring for paradigm, and the adolescents will eventually grow into young adults.

HOW TO DEAL
WITH YOUNG ADULTS

The crucial management method with people in this stage is to encourage their interest in and use of processes. It's not sufficient to receive goals and action plans from them. You want them to articulate the how and why behind those goals and plans. One effective technique is to ask your people to develop rationales for doing something one way as opposed to another. This helps them think in process terms—the same terms they're thinking in as young parents.

Unlike the adolescent group, young adults don't respond well to ultimatums. They require discussion about why something should be done. Adolescents, of course, ask *why* to test adults. The only rational response to that test is to make sure they know you're serious and instruct them to do it. Young adults, however, require explanations because they really want to understand the process behind an action. If organizations want to build strong cultures, their managers will supply the whys and wherefores. More than any other group, young adults build cultures, and they should be given every opportunity to build strong ones.

HOW TO DEAL WITH ADULTS

These people push values through organizations. They are the ones who recognize the importance of value clarification and value consistency. As adults, they can appreciate the need for values whereas adolescents can't; this is why boards of directors talk about mission and purpose and junior managers talk about dates and working out. But even adults won't drive values unless management helps them solidify the link between the personal and the professional.

It is this group that can most benefit from the new paradigm: *Who we are personally is inextricably connected to who we are professionally; the goal is to lead blended, not balanced, lives.* In fact, the strength of a company's value-based management apparatus is determined by the blended lives of its adult employees. When they keep the personal and professional separate, values become fuzzy or low risk. An older executive who is just marking time until retirement is often let out to pasture; management assumes that he is simply tired of work. In fact, the problem is personal, not professional. The sixty-two-year-old executive who says he can't stand to think about attending another strategic planning meeting and longs to escape his boring routine is really saying, "I've lost my purpose in life; I no longer have a personal mission." He has no idea how his participation in a strategic planning meeting relates to what he's all about. But when he thinks about how boring work is, he never thinks about it in personal terms.

Neither does his boss.   When managers attempt to reenergize these seemingly burned-out cases, they make the mistake of focusing on work; they try to motivate such people with money. These people often respond, "I don't need to make more money."

Instead, the focus should start with the personal. A sales manager might ask a salesperson, "What do you really want to get out of the next ten years of your life; not your work life, but what do you really want to accomplish, what would get you interested and excited?"

The salesperson might respond, "Well, I used to really like getting people interested in what I'm interested in. That used to be exciting, but it's not anymore."

The sales manager might then point out that the missing excitement isn't because of the usual reasons—a less attractive product line, more demanding customers, new and irritating corporate policies—but because he no longer has any idea about why he works. The sales manager might then add that the reason people work is not to make a sale but to engage in a relationship, and his old method of building relationships no longer works. After acknowledging his salesperson's disappointment about this fact, he might suggest that he can learn a new method of establishing relationships.

"I don't know if I want to learn a new way," the salesperson might complain. The sales manager would reply; "Is it that you don't want to or don't understand how to? If it's the latter, you have a great opportunity to learn."

When personal and professional issues are integrated, values are more easily clarified. If the salesperson realizes that his boredom at work is inextricably connected to the lack of a personal mission in life, he begins to view himself holistically—he's no longer split into personal and professional selfs. When that happens, adults can start working toward value confluence in all aspects of their lives.

Value-confluent adults are not only tremendously productive, but they solidify company values. From an adult point of view, anyone can make widgets. What makes Company A different from Company B are values. Company A doesn't just want to make widgets; it wants to make them the right way. These values infuse a company's culture and help it stand out in a cluttered marketplace. In addition, both employees and customers are attracted to the values espoused by Company A. They want to be associated with an organization where people are constantly growing and learning about themselves.

THE GRAY AREAS

The three stages I've described in this chapter aren't as clear-cut in reality as they might appear on the page. For instance, someone might start a family at thirty and begin acting like a young adult, but she might also retain some adolescent behaviors, hovering in the gray areas between stages. A fifty-five-year-old manager who has been in the adult stage for years gets divorced and suddenly starts acting like an adolescent, cruising and bar-hopping.

Regressing from one stage to another happens, and companies shouldn't be overly alarmed if their people repeat stages. They should be alarmed when people get stuck in stages. If that fifty-five-year-old manager continues her adolescent behavior of one indiscriminate relationship after another for long periods, there's a problem. The solution is not to indulge or excuse this behavior. It's not harmless behavior, either to herself or the company. Someone needs to make her aware that her actions aren't positive and will prevent her from making a contribution to her life or to the company.

THREE REQUIREMENTS FOR MANAGING STAGES

Every organization can manage the delayed development of its people—especially its adolescent employees—if it focuses on the following three imperatives:

- **Reparent the workforce.** When I ask middle-aged managers what life experiences they had before they were in their twenties, many respond with marriage, kids, serving in the military. Now very few employees have gone through any of those experiences prior to entering the workforce. Companies need to be acutely aware that their younger people require reparenting— the guidance, rules, and policies developed by those with the requisite experience. This translates into setting clear expectations and consequences; it means employing the conflict, confrontation, and challenge of the caring for model. However, the parental style used to deal with these employees must accommodate the four unbreakable rules discussed on pages 150-151. Be unambiguous and consistent, but refrain from lecturing.

- **Provide consistent feedback and predictable consequences.** Adolescents will test adults in all sorts of ways, and the only way to respond is with consistency. Young employees need to know how you'll respond if they come in late or if they miss a deadline; they need to know what the rewards and punishments are for certain types of behavior. The goal is to create a growth orientation for adolescents rather than a comfort orientation. Predictable and consistent consequences facilitate their growth, whereas unpredictable and inconsistent actions allow them to remain both comfortable and dysfunctional.

- **Serve as models for competent adult behavior.** In the days when employees gained experience earlier in their lives, they could more easily dismiss bizarre or negative behavior on the part of senior managers. As young adults, they had acquired a measure of maturity and were not as easily influenced by such models. But adolescents pay great attention to the actions of role models. When management lectures about responsibility and the perils of addiction and the adolescent's boss has three drinks in the middle of the day, the contradiction is impossible to ignore or reconcile.

CHAPTER

ACCOUNTABILITY: THE SEVEN PREREQUISITES

12

A corporation working without a net is not a solo act. Survival depends on the ability of employees to work with each other to accomplish goals. If the employees cannot depend on each other, or are working at cross-purposes, chaos and crises result. In this chapter and the next one, we will be looking at accountability and goals—two values essential for success in a high risk culture.

THE VALUE OF ACCOUNTABILITY

As much as we may like to think that accountability exists in our workplace, we usually have nothing of the kind. Instead we've installed an ersatz version of this value. Organizations give the concept lip service, but they're reluctant to hold anyone truly accountable. They're reluctant because of the drive for comfort in our society; confrontation and conflict are often required to hold people accountable, and many managers would prefer to avoid making their subordinates and themselves uncomfortable. Once again we see the caretaking paradigm as a handicap in the high risk culture.

Accountable organizations, on the other hand, are successful, productive ones. When accountability is structured into work set-

157

tings and relationships, employees more quickly assume adult behaviors, and the value-based management system so necessary in these high risk times becomes stronger. To foster accountability in your workplace, the following seven prerequisites are necessary. Let's examine each of them and see how you can make them part of your culture.

1. Accountability is to individuals; not to groups, committees, or organizations

Perhaps the biggest myth about accountability is that it can exist outside of one-to-one relationships. In many companies, you'll hear people talking about how they're accountable to a project team or a department; you'll find an adolescent employee who proclaims that he's going to get something done because his department is counting on him.

But you can't look the department in the eye and say you didn't do it; the department won't tell you it's disappointed in you and that there will be consequences for not completing the assigned task.

Dyadic (one-to-one) relationships personalize accountability. They ensure that one person has a vested interest in the other person doing something. Of course, individual accountability is more difficult to institute and maintain than group accountability because it leads to conflict and confrontation, which is also psychologically and emotionally uncomfortable. But without a personalized approach, you give people an accountability escape clause. When someone doesn't have a single person who expects her to complete a job on time or in a certain way, she will not feel compelled to do so.

When people try to implement one-to-one accountability, however, they encounter two roadblocks:

- First, there's the prevailing philosophy that "this is business; don't make it personal." People who harbor this sentiment equate personal accountability with hostility. To them, making it personal means ad hominem attacks. In fact, they're mistaking confrontation and conflict for hostility. The personal approach becomes palatable when we realize it doesn't require us to be mean and nasty.

- The other roadblock is a nonhierarchical organization. The quest to drive decision-making down to the lowest levels and democratize companies through flattening structures obviates accountability. In flattened organizations where everyone is equal and consensus is key, there is little or no conflict, confrontations, or accountability. Without the personal leverage that hierarchical organizations provide, accountability is a hollow and meaningless word.

2. Clarify the areas in which one will be held accountable

The two areas in which we hold people accountable are *macro* (or value) and *micro* (or functional). Most organizations pay a good deal of attention to the latter and very little attention to the former. They frequently fail to sit down with people and detail the behaviors, activities, and attitudes that must be consonant with the organization's values. As a result, employees assume that they'll be held accountable only for the functional tasks and skills related to their jobs; that they're accountable only for what they do, not how they do it. A manager may be trained and held accountable for meeting sales goals, but he's not held accountable for the slave-driving approach he uses on his people to meet those goals.

MACRO

We ignore these macro areas because they make us uncomfortable. Although it's easy to tell someone he doesn't type sufficiently fast, it's difficult to tell him that his attitude is intolerable. In addition, management has generally felt it had no right to intrude in the area of employee attitudes; that it was somehow forbidden ground.

Employee attitudes, behaviors, and activities, however, can have a profound impact on business. For instance, a client of mine was checking into a Ritz-Carlton hotel late at night and saw an elderly couple struggling with their luggage across the lobby. No doorman or bellboy was around, but a Ritz Carlton employee who was washing the windows climbed down from his ladder, helped them carry their luggage to the registration desk, and asked if there was anything else he could do for them. My client then went over to the window washer and asked him if he was also the bellboy. The window washer said no but that the mission of Ritz Carlton is always meet the needs of its customers, and that everyone pitches in to meet those needs, no matter what his or her particular job is. My client noted that the window washer really seemed to enjoy helping the elderly couple.

MICRO

Though I emphasize the importance of the macro, I don't mean to suggest that the micro is insignificant. All employees need to be held accountable in the following four micro areas:

- Technical or content competence. In other words, people must meet the role expectations of their jobs.

- Business acumen and knowledge. Are employees just putting in time or using their time profitably? People need to be held accountable for involving themselves in profit-making activities; they shouldn't hide behind routine paperwork all day when they could help complete a money-making project.

- Sales and marketing ability. This accountability area isn't just for sales or marketing people. Everyone in an organization is in a direct or indirect sales role. Even if you never deal directly with customers, you work with other employees who do. The more you can help them with their jobs, the better they can sell and market. Companies don't have the luxury of keeping certain jobs pristine—free of the nitty-gritty responsibilities of selling.

- Communication and interpersonal skills. It's not enough to achieve results. Being aware of and learning from the process that gets results is crucial. Some people may find solutions for customers, but they deliver those solutions in obnoxious or irritating ways. Customers will eventually jettison relationships with obnoxious and difficult people, no matter how many problems they solve.

3. Expectations must be stated in a specific and clearly differentiating manner

When it comes to fostering accountability, we have a responsibility to tell people what we expect from them. They generally respond that they intend to meet those expectations, but their behaviors remain the same. The guiding principle for this prerequisite, therefore, is:

Unless new behavior is exhibited, no learning has taken place and no accountability will result.

We let people get away with murder because they make great protestations about their intentions to change. Accountability, however, is not about intent to change but about achievement of different results.

To avoid this problem,

- Define precisely what new behaviors must be seen and exhibited.

- Define precisely what old behaviors must be abandoned and not seen.

The operative word is *precisely*. The more specific we are in laying out our expectations, the more likely people's behaviors will change to meet them.

Most of us, however, become involved in games of escalating protestations. For instance, a manager tells his subordinate that the next time he deals with client Jim, he shouldn't be so pushy and controlling. The subordinate agrees and says he won't act that way anymore. Yet during his next meeting with Jim, he is as pushy and controlling as always. The manager again talks to his subordinate, and his subordinate apologizes profusely and is sincere and convincing when he says he'll back off when dealing with Jim. Yet nothing changes. The manager goes through the routine of giving his subordinate "one more chance." Then he gives him another chance after that.

Underneath this apparent spinelessness lurks the old and outmoded paradigm about change, the one that says people can't change, and you shouldn't expect them to. Remember these paradigms: (1) *People's ability to change is not a function of capacity but of choice, and,* (2) *we need to change our attitudes toward change.* The new change paradigm must reinforce all efforts to instill accountability in the workplace. Expect stress, expect confrontation, and understand that these are normal parts of the change process.

To prevent employees from endlessly dodging and postponing change, get specific. In fact, it sometimes helps to get specific to the point that you "script" a possible interaction. For instance, a sales manager wants a salesperson to make points more quickly because her longwinded explanations are driving customers away. If he simply says, "I expect you to talk less," the salesperson might reduce her presentations by a few seconds, but still be perceived as rambling and obtuse. But the sales manager can instead try this approach: "I want you to give customers only the information that disturbs them and gets their attention. As soon as you see you've done that, be quiet and listen. The first sign of disturbance is when they tell you they can't do what you want; it costs too much."

Banish all generalities when telling your people what you expect. Don't fall back on old favorites like, "You have to have a better attitude" or "We expect you to be more productive." Translate what those generalities mean: "You have to smile more, establish eye contact, eliminate that sneer, don't evade tough questions."

Finally, manage conflict around these expectations. In other words, make sure you obtain buy-in upfront from your people and deal at the time with whatever conflict that request for a buy-in causes. If a conflict exists, bring it out in the open immediately. If you don't deal with it upfront, it will thwart the achievement of your stated expectations. It's also possible that you won't receive a buy-in—an employee refuses to go along with what you expect him to do. In this instance, serious consideration must be given to whether the employee belongs with your organization.

4. Measurement of expectations must delineate quantity and time frame

This prerequisite translates into, "You need to tell people how much change is expected and how you're going to measure it." Telling a number of individuals that their presentations should be shorter won't have much effect. You need to tell them that their presentations can't last longer than ten minutes; that they should limit the number of issues they discuss to three; that if during their next presentation they don't meet those expectations, they won't be allowed to do any more presentations. In this instance, the amount of change that you expect is clear, as is your measurement standard.

The next requirement is setting deadlines for change to be accomplished. More than any other accountability issue, this is the one with which managers have the most trouble. Most of you have attended meetings in which great plans were made and everyone left the meeting enthusiastic, excited, and convinced that major changes were ahead. But nothing ever happened because no time frames were ever mentioned. They probably weren't mentioned because time frames establish the ultimate accountability and potentially the ultimate confrontation. Deadlines remove plans and agreements from the realm of fantasy. When time frames are set, there is a real and immediate consequence for not completing a task. Low risk managers shy away from putting themselves on these collision courses with employees.

All this doesn't mean that you should become rigid about how due dates are set. In other words, don't demand that a project be completed in two weeks and refuse to listen to an employee's explanation of why that's an unreasonable time frame. When setting deadlines, high risk managers are sufficiently flexible that they're willing to negotiate due dates with employees. In fact, such negotiating can help some employees become more sincerely committed to the change and cause them to feel personal responsibility for making it.

MEASUREMENTS OF CARING

Some people immediately respond with negativity to talk of deadlines and measurements. For them, it translates into hounding of, spying on, and distrust of employees. Certainly deadlines and measurements can be misused—an absurd deadline is given to harass someone the company wants to get rid of, for instance. But used properly, measurements and time frames are forms of caring. You measure people's performance to tell them how they're doing and what they can do better. If you didn't measure them, you'd essentially be saying, "I don't really care how you do, and I'm not giving you a time frame because I don't think you have the capability to finish the job in any reasonable period of time." This caretaking stance is antithetical to accountability.

Sports provides us with a good analogy for this prerequisite. We want coaches to measure the teams and professional athletes we root for. We don't want coaches to give athletes unconditional acceptance. Imagine if Michael Jordan's coaches had told him, "It's okay, Michael, you don't have to practice shooting or rebounding or free throws. You're a great guy, so we're not going to force you to do anything you don't want to do.´ We want coaches to set parameters: doing a certain number of laps each day, a certain amount of weightlifting, and so on. A coach who didn't set any of these measures sends a message that she doesn't care about the team or the individuals on it.

Just as troubling, a lack of measures catalyzes rebellion and passive-aggressive behavior, particularly in today's developmentally delayed employee. Like children, people who lack the limits that measures provide become scared. They act out to tell management that "we don't know what you expect of us and we want to get your attention by being a problem for you."

5. Consequences for meeting or failing to meet established expectations must be stated in detail

Accountability is facilitated when we state *both* the positive and negative consequences. Offering only positive or negative consequences is like giving employees only half of the reason why they should be accountable.

In addition, the negative consequences should neither be general nor repeated. When people possess only a vague sense of what will happen if they fail to meet expectations, they aren't particularly motivated to change their behavior. Similarly, the same consequence repeated ad infinitum quickly loses its impact. One of the most common repeated consequences—yelling at people and issuing the same threat—has the identical effect on employees as on children constantly yelled at by parents: They build up a tolerance for being screamed at.

A multi-stage, escalating series of negative consequences is an effective facet of an accountability strategy. Such a series is more effective than the same consequences repeated again and again, and ensures that employees know exactly what will happen if they fail to meet expectations. Though there is no perfect number of stages, the final one should always be termination. Here's a sample series for an employee who arrives late for work:

1. Conference with manager, who will warn the employee that lateness is prohibited and note the warning in the employee's file
2. Employee put on notice via a written document
3. Loss of pay for the day when the employee arrives late
4. Termination

Some organizations, on the other hand, make exceptions for the quietly mediocre. They allow them to escape the consequences that apply to others. These employees are given passes because they never raise a stink and they don't make any demands. Though they're not particularly productive, they've usually been around for a while and it seems more trouble than it's worth to make them accountable. The problem with these exceptions is that they model stagnation for the rest of the organization. You lose your credibility when you make exceptions, especially with an adolescent employee population. When these employees see that low productivity is acceptable, many will comfortably settle into an "adequate" mode, and stagnation will spread. To implement another essential new paradigm introduced in Chapter 2—*redefine what constitutes acceptable work; move from adequacy to peak performance*—you must allow no exceptions in accountability. Accountability suffers when you provide an alternative to high expectations.

Similarly, accountability is difficult to achieve when your consequences are meekly presented—or, to put it more bluntly, when you fail to use fear as a motivator. Contrary to common belief, fear is a healthy motivator. Many people wouldn't drive at the speed limit or pay their taxes if it weren't for their fear of the consequences. Many couples remain monogamous despite their natural attraction to others; they do so because they are afraid that affairs would disappoint and hurt their partners. When fear is part of a respectful personal or professional relationship, it is a healthy emotion. It's only when two people have no respect that fear turns unhealthy. When a boss views his employees as mindless slaves, for instance, fear is used solely for the purposes of intimidation.

6. Consequences must be enacted with immediacy, objectivity, and clarity

How you set consequences is just as important as what those consequences entail. They have to be articulated and set into action in certain ways.

The first way is to enact consequences immediately after a person fails to meet an expectation. If you wait days or weeks to talk to a subordinate about his unacceptable behavior, he will discount or misinterpret what you're telling him. You've lost the clear cause-and-effect relationship between his action and your consequence. Elapsed time severs that relationship, and as a result the subordinate assumes that you have a hidden agenda behind your admonition. He thinks that you're being critical of him because you don't like him or you're in a bad mood. Delaying your delivery of the consequence is akin to hitting a dog on the nose a week after he used your favorite rug as a toilet; he won't have any understanding of the real reason for your action.

Second, you need to deliver the consequence in a calm, nonreactive manner. Some managers scream or take undue pleasure in chastising subordinates. This directs attention to the emotional content of the approach—the real message is obfuscated and people don't focus on what they did wrong. Calm managers confront whereas hot-tempered ones are hostile. You want your people to concentrate on the substance of the message and not the style.

Third, clarify consequences so that there's no confusion about the choices that produced those consequences. People come up with great excuses or mitigating circumstances when they fail to meet expectations. Don't accept them, and don't let your people accept them either. When they continually arrive late to work because "traffic is terrible and I can't control traffic," the appropriate response is, "You don't control traffic, but you control the time you leave for work. You've made a choice that there are more important things than getting to work on time." Our organizations, however, indulge excuse making and often adapt environments to certain employees' mitigating circumstances—everyone who lives ten miles away can come in ten minutes late; parents with babies can work at home; each department is governed by a different policy. No wonder employees are so adept at manipulating management.

7. Accountability must be consistently modeled by top management

Top managers have to hold themselves accountable in the same way that they hold others accountable. Adolescent employees are desperately looking for models who are consistent both in terms of functional behavior and values. If a CEO stresses openness and toleration but is known as someone who will "get you" if you dare to argue with him, the inconsistency will destroy his worth as a model.

There's a lot of superficiality related to this issue. I've seen executives who claim to "walk the talk," but in reality they have done nothing more than give up their reserved parking spaces or undertaken a token flattening of the organization. These are empty, symbolic gestures. Consistently modeling accountability is a twenty-four-hour, seven-day-a-week job. A number of CEOs have shared with me the difficulty of being ruthlessly consistent. They wish they could knock down four or five drinks after a tough day with their management teams or not be among the first ones in the office every day. But they're also aware that workers will be tempted to use any inconsistency as a reason not to be accountable.

THE ACCOUNTABILITY TEST

Asking the following questions will help you determine how effective accountability is for you, your group, and your organization:

- In your area of responsibility, who holds whom accountable for the work to be done?

- Between your area and another area, who holds whom accountable?

Ideally, your organization will be able to create a list in which every employee holds one other employee accountable. In dysfunctional organizations, people answer these questions with the names of departments, teams, small groups, and even the corporate entity; or they answer with the names of two or three different supervisors, the classic split-supervision model that dilutes accountability.

If you or your organization is unable to answer with one-on-one accountability, the first prerequisite is where you need to start. Once you've achieved this structural accountability, implement the other six prerequisites.

Implementation should be as proactive as possible. By that I mean you shouldn't approach accountability as something you do in response to a specific problem. Companies often resort to accountability when they find that entire departments aren't meeting the objectives they set forth or individual employees are violating verbal agreements with their superiors. As a result, these companies end up teaching their people how to be accountable only in very specific situations. They don't inculcate accountability into the culture. The ideal scenario is for employees to be acculturated with this notion of accountability from the moment they join the organization.

A CARING FOR MODEL

I can't overemphasize the need for accountability. Without it, growth doesn't take place. Accountability provides the structure for growth and development, which I'll talk about in more detail later. For now, recognize that the negative connotations of accountability—that it's the whip used by sadistic managers to torture employees—are false. In fact, when managers don't hold their people accountable, they're abandoning them, and nothing could be more cruel than that action. In every organization, accountability provides an essential function: shaping individuals as they grow, develop, and form as responsible adults.

CHAPTER
GOALS
AND
ACCOUNTABILITY

The preceding chapter discussed establishing a system of accountability. Accountability is what you need to accomplish goals. Goals are what you need to realize peak performance. Peak performance is what you and your organization need to survive and thrive without a net.

Until we've inculcated the seven prerequisites from the previous chapter into our organizations and our lives, we won't be able to establish goals. Many companies not only lack these prerequisites, they don't understand why they set goals in the first place. Goal setting has become a perfunctory exercise, a quotidian part of the organizational routine. Every day millions of businesspeople set millions of goals that will never be accomplished; or, if accomplished, contribute little to the growth of the corporation or the individual. This occurs because those millions of businesspeople don't have a clue about why they've set those goals.

Let's examine the role of goals and how individuals and organizations can set and achieve them effectively.

REASSURING LIMITS

Discipline serves the same purpose for children that goals do for adults. Both provide feelings of safety and security in a frightening, uncertain world. Children will not develop in a climate where they are allowed to do whatever they want; such a climate produces anxiety at first and, if it continues, terror. Kids need to know the lines they can't cross; they need to understand what's safe and what's unsafe. If you've ever watched a child in a playground, you'll understand what I'm talking about. Young children who go to playgrounds with their parents engage in a seemingly choreographed ballet—they play on the equipment, run to parents and touch them for a moment, then return to the playground, repeating this back-and-forth dance often. They return to parents to reestablish the boundaries; once they've done that, they feel sufficiently secure to go out on their own for a little while.

Goals establish the same type of boundaries for adults by establishing parameters for action. Goals limit your options in the short term in order to expand them in the long term; they give you a path; they prevent you from dissipating energy and resources to no useful purpose. Goals enable you to bring strength, order, and momentum into the unpredictable and frightening marketplace. If an organization's goal is to serve its market segment of upscale young adults to the best of its ability, its strategy and tactics will be defined by that goal. Without it, strategy and tactics become unfocused. When companies diversify into areas outside of their goals, they get into trouble. For instance, in the 1980s a number of national retailers diversified into real estate, the stock brokerage business, and other areas. Their major goal—meeting the needs of retail customers—became fuzzy, and they lost money prodigiously. Most of those retailers have now sold off their nonretail businesses.

SETTING LIMITS
TO PROMOTE GROWTH

Individual goals serve the same function as organizational ones. Early in one's career, they're especially important. A supervisor may tell her young assistant, "Your goal for the next year is to develop as many contacts in our field as you possibly can." The young assistant may protest that he needs to develop technical skills or that he has to do a lot of research. The supervisor may then reply, "This business is a game of numbers, and no amount of technical skills or knowledge of the field will help you like contacts will. So that is your only goal." Certainly that goal is limiting but only temporarily. It also provides the young assistant with a measure of safety; the boundaries are clearly drawn. He can focus all his time and energy on one thing and not be distracted or confused by all the other possibilities around him.

Both in our personal and professional lives, we're frequently overwhelmed by opportunities, impulses, and feelings. We try to learn five different skills simultaneously and end up doing justice to none of them. Or we go after ten prospects when we should be concentrating on the best one. Goals provide us with an automatic selection process, enabling us to pursue the most productive course of action.

Some people are skeptical about the need for boundaries. The legacy of the 1960s is the notion that limits are limiting; that total freedom yields total creativity. Anyone burdened by this notion should do two things: See one particular movie and have kids. The movie is *Altered States*. On the basis of early space research designed to test the physiological effects of a weightless and pressureless environment, the film focused on the psychological effects revealed by the experiments. It demonstrated that when the test subject was put into a chamber where all sensory input was removed, the experience drove the subject crazy. With no sensory references to delineate himself, the subject became clinically psychotic.

Similarly, if you were to tell children that today they can do everything they want to do, they would grind to a halt. Though they may want to do everything, they are unable to handle the opportunity to do so.

For children, the answer is an authority figure who sets clear limits. For adults, the answer is setting clear goals.

SETTING GOALS

The first lesson about setting goals is that most people achieve goals, celebrate, and then try to reset their goals. Instead, they need to reset their goals before they celebrate.

People are most vulnerable to failure when they reach their goals, not when they're working toward them. What typically happens is that once they accomplish what they set out to do, they celebrate and postpone resetting goals. Companies that land a big customer, experience a terrific quarter, or have a successful new product introduction invariably follow those up periods with down ones. This rollercoaster syndrome is caused by the unannounced vacation people take when they've achieved their goals. They start coasting, forgetting to make calls they normally would make, delaying new projects, and generally taking it easy. They pay for their inattention when they experience a sudden drop. Only then do they realize they should come up with some new goals.

To avoid this rollercoaster ride, reset goals the moment you achieve an objective.

THREE TYPES OF GOALS

Setting goals is a comprehensive, holistic process. It's not the limited, selective activity many presume it to be. Perhaps the best example of this point relates to a paradigm that's run throughout these pages: the blending of the personal and the professional. If you create great work relationship goals but ignore your personal relationship goals, dissonance will be created. As admirable and ambitious as your customer and coworker relationship goals are, you won't achieve them without similarly admirable and ambitious personal relationship goals.

An example of a personal relationship goal might be to deal effectively with the time-consuming needs of two sets of in-laws. Another goal might be to resolve the differences between you and your spouse about how you discipline your children. At first blush, these goals might seem unrelated to your goals at work. But as you've seen and will continue to see throughout this book, they're one and the same.

Not only do these two sets of goals need to blend, but they also need to track with a third set: self-improvement goals. This category of goals usually is viewed simplistically: "I should take a course in subject x"; or, "I'm going to start reading three books a week about field y." Self-improvement goals won't be meaningful unless they meet the following criteria:

- The area of improvement is one that you know little about or have no particular skills in.

- The area of improvement scares you.

Most people choose areas they're comfortable with—business people who go back to school to get MBAs, for instance. They improve a little bit, but the fear and the knowledge gap that would drive them to make improvement leaps are missing. If you're afraid and lack necessary knowledge, your focus is greatly sharpened and you're capable of much more learning and growth.

For instance, a few years back I was bothered that I wasn't as good as and didn't know as much as I could have about concentration and focus. When I had to get something done that wasn't a top priority, I would become easily distracted. I wanted to improve my concentration, and I found an unusual vehicle for doing so. As the owner of a sports car, I had always had a certain interest in racing. But I knew very little about the sport of race car driving, and the prospect of learning how to race my car on a competition track frightened me. So I enrolled in a race car driving school. When I arrived, I saw these men bent over the engines of their cars, looking as if they knew exactly what they were doing. I didn't even know how to change the oil in my car. Yet it was a phenomenal experience. I learned that racing has little to do with mechanical ability or raw speed. The drivers who win races don't go significantly faster than their competition; they drive better. I learned that drivers are among the most focused people in the world. If I lost focus for a second behind the wheel, my instructor would jump on me immediately. You can't afford to lose focus going through a curve at 80 miles per hour.

Once I completed the course, my concentration in a number of areas in my life greatly improved. The payoff was a result of my fear and complete lack of knowledge. If I had taken a seminar guaranteed to improve my powers of concentration, the payoff would never have been as great.

YOUR PERSONAL MISSION

Goal setting is only meaningful if you possess a personal mission that unifies and drives your personal and professional lives. Many people lack this mission and therefore lack the commitment necessary to achieve ambitious goals. Understanding what someone's personal mission is can be a bit tricky. It's not always easily glimpsed based on the jobs people have. For instance, I've done a number of very different things in my career. I started as a professor of cultural history; I opened a practice as a psychotherapist; I worked with educators and law enforcement officers on issues of stress and organizational planning; I became a corporate consultant. On the surface, these four jobs look very dissimilar. But the underlying mission behind everything I've done is teaching. In each position, the driving force was to help people improve the personal and professional quality of their lives by teaching them more about who they are. Because of that mission, my commitment was high, and I achieved my goals.

When I ask people what their missions are, their responses are usually three or four levels removed from their missions. They usually describe something that has to do with making a living. For instance, "I'm an internist because I derive great satisfaction from helping sick people feel better." Then why is this person an internist and not a nurse, a chiropractor, or a surgeon? When I ask a retailer why he does what he does, he responds, "I do it because I like being around people." But he could be around people if he was a social worker or a teacher. You have to dig deeper to find your mission.

To dig deeper, ask yourself the following questions:

1. Why do you do what you do? (Your reasons can't simply stop at making a living and should revolve around nonmonetary issues.)
2. What impact do you want to make on a group of people as a result of the job you do?

You may want to answer the second question first, using it as a probe to get beneath the surface of why you do what you do. For instance, a financial planner might respond that the impact she wants to make on her clients is to open their eyes to all the options available to them; that with sound financial planning they can explore alternate careers and lifestyles that they may not have thought they could afford to pursue. For her, financial planning is just a vehicle to achieve her larger mission of helping people think creatively about their options.

Without this unifying mission, you won't achieve many goals of significance. Highly successful people—especially highly successful businesspeople—are visionaries. Rather than looking at what they do and why they do it in nuts-and-bolts terms, they possess a powerful vision that drives them.

WHAT CORE VALUE SYSTEM DRIVES YOU?

If you have trouble articulating why you do what you do—at least articulating it in the way I've suggested—the problem may reside with your values. Core values drive mission statements. People who achieve their goals have a clear correspondence between their values and their mission. To help you determine if you have that correspondence, consider your responses to the value clarification instrument. As you'll recall, you determined whether you were high-risk, low-risk, or value confused relative to the three core values: responsibility, change, and reward/payoff. The following exercise will help you look at your values as they relate to your mission and goals:

* Define each of the three core values in your own words.

Write your definitions on a piece of paper using your own words and feelings. Use the following prompts if you'd like:

* What does responsibility mean in your life; what does it mean to be responsible?

* How do you see change affecting your life; how should change affect other people's lives?

* What reward do you want; what options are you striving to develop?

A high-risk sales rep might answer the responsibility question by writing, "Responsibility means showing customers that they can do much more with our products and services than they ever thought. Instead of allowing them to underutilize what we give them and to search high and low for solutions, my charge is to show them how they can draw on their own resources and our products and services to solve problems."

A low-risk sales rep, however, might answer the responsibility question by writing, "My responsibility is to sell as many of our products to customers as I can and maintain an amiable relationship with them so that they continue to want to do business with me." This employee's views on responsibility are much less sharply focused. He has a short-term responsibility to please his employer by meeting or exceeding a sales quota, but his attitude is unlikely to create a competitive advantage for his company because he's exhibiting classical caretaking behavior. This schmoozer will eventually lose sales to a company that's more transactional than his own.

After you've defined each of the core values in your own words, answer the following:

- Are your three definitions compatible or do they clash?

For instance, how does your view of responsibility relate to your view of change? Will your definition of responsibility be accomplished if people follow your definition of change? If so, are they compatible with your reward/payoff definition—why you're working where you're working?

Let's say your idea of responsibility is to enhance people's ability to make decisions in their lives. Do you work for a company that encourages *you* to do that? Or is it an organization that wants its people to be wholly dependent on management's decision making? If it's the latter, you're going to be frustrated because there's a clash with your responsibility core value. It's not that the actual work is wrong for you, but you have an internal value conflict. Setting and achieving goals in the face of this conflict is impossible. All you're doing is inviting early burnout.

Let's assume your concept of responsibility is to help people deal with the long-term issues in their lives. As a counselor with a diet center, however, you find that management instructs you to simply harangue dieters about their eating habits and calories consumed. Management wants you to focus on short-term behaviors that only result in temporary weight loss. You believe that permanent weight loss is only possible if your clients make long-term changes in their lives. Consequently, you don't feel as if you're doing meaningful work. You lack a sense of mission because of the internal value conflict and can't accomplish your goals.

Do all three of your core values coexist peacefully? If they're diametrically opposed, you'll fall short of your goals. Many people do what they do simply to pay the bills. When you get to the root of why you do what you do, however, you can both pay the bills and satisfy your values. That's where the visionary zeal of the most successful businesspeople comes from.

I'll end this chapter by summarizing the linkages between values, mission, and goals. Value clarity allows you to set and achieve goals. Your coherent value system helps you establish a mission, which in turn drives you toward your goals.

PART FOUR
CONFLICT, ANGER, AND LOYALTY

CHAPTER

FIVE STEPS TO CONFLICT MANAGEMENT

14

It would be wonderful if instilling accountability and goals was as simple as installing a new program into a computer. But we're working with human beings, not computers, and so the process is a lot messier. Talk of accountability and goals makes some people defensive. They may feel as if they haven't been performing up to expectations and that they've been found lacking. Or, they may feel they've been doing a perfectly good job but management doesn't understand. In these cases, conflict is just around the corner.

When you talk to employees about goals, for example, you're focusing on who they are and what they want to accomplish. Such talk often causes them to react defensively; they don't want to deal with issues that hit so close to home. As a result, these employees generate conflict. Other employees become embroiled in the argument and distracted from the original goal-related subject.

From a managerial point of view, the issue is whether you're going to manage that conflict or allow it to become a distraction from what you want to accomplish. When conflict manifests itself as an argument, everything becomes secondary to the argument. The focus shifts away from the original point of the discussion and toward who is going to win the argument. It's very difficult to get back to that original point after you've come to verbal blows with someone. Even if the matter is resolved, the emotions stirred up by the dispute linger. A manager and a subordinate who have just engaged in a furious debate over some petty issue will forget all about their initial topic of how the subordinate can set and accomplish personal and professional goals.

Managing conflict is an essential process for any manager. Before helping you learn that process, we need to dispel some common misconceptions about conflict.

CONFLICT VERSUS HOSTILITY

Conflict isn't negative. Most people see it as a nasty, abrasive, hostile interaction. Conflict, however, has nothing to do with these negative traits. Conflict involves a clash in perceptions and expectations, neither of which have been properly articulated. Hostility, on the other hand, is a conflict-avoidance mechanism. Hostility occurs when people globalize issues; they make sweeping generalizations and attack individuals. For example, when a new manager chastises an old sales rep about his expense accounts, the rep becomes hostile. He's done his job as he sees it, but instead of being rewarded he's being punished. The rep's self-perceptions are on the line: He's a pro, and he knows how the game is played. This neophyte manager hasn't put in her time out on the road that he has. As a result, he clings to the old routine and becomes defensive. The manager, on the other hand, views this guy as a throwback to the Fuller Brush salesman who can't see the big picture. She feels he's too stuck in the past to learn new approaches. Instead of trying to help him change, she looks for the first opportunity to move him into a less promising territory where he can do little damage.

These tactics are convenient distractions and diversions. *Hostile people don't want to resolve issues.*

RESOLVING THE REAL ISSUES

The object of conflict management is to bring clashing perceptions and expectations into harmony. Most organizations are not particularly adept at this task. They're not adept because conflict management is about feelings; organizations are much more comfortable with thought-related activities.

Our companies are filled with hostile people who use thoughts as weapons and their wit like machetes. It's not a coincidence that some of our brightest and most articulate people are so hostile, because hostility is intimately tied to thought processes. We use thoughts—she's just another no-brain manager; he's an old fool who can't see the big picture—to avoid dealing with (and taking responsibility for) our feelings. Conflict management, although it involves thoughts, is equally a feeling process. It gets feelings out on the table so they can be dealt with. It enables you to frame and articulate the feelings in an interaction so they're understandable to people. It also allows people to work through a process that resolves seemingly disparate feelings and get to the point where they can deal with the resolution. This doesn't mean that one person gets his way, but that both people have acknowledged and talked about their feelings and related issues.

The following are the five steps of the conflict management process:

- Clarifying discrepancies

- Setting expectations

- Defining limits and boundaries

- Taking ownership of choices

- Making a decision

STEP ONE: ## CLARIFYING DISCREPANCIES

This is the first and most important step of the process because 90 percent of the time people argue about the wrong issue. On the surface, a boss is arguing with his subordinate about whether the subordinate deserves a raise, but the real issue involves the subordinate's belief that his values are not respected and validated by the company. When underlying issues aren't dealt with, people become frustrated, fail, and eventually burn out.

The discrepancy between surface and underlying issues is easily seen in feuding couples. They regularly fight about who does the dishes, who takes out the garbage, who drives the kids. Their fights are patterned. In other words, they occur at approximately the same time at night—usually between 7:00 and 10:00. When I would meet with these couples as a clinician, I learned that they didn't have the faintest idea why they were arguing three nights in a row about who should take out the garbage. To help them get at the underlying issue, I'd ask them when the arguments occurred and how they made them feel. Couples would respond that arguments almost always came up in the evening and left them feeling that they wanted nothing to do with each other. It was logical to conclude that the purpose of the fights was to eliminate the potential for intimacy. These couples were freaked out by intimacy. They never talked about closeness or their sexuality and dealt with it obliquely by arguing about superficial issues.

The same sort of thing goes on in the business environment, albeit with different manifestations. I have often worked with successful business leaders who are considered aloof and uncaring. Because of their posture, they engender conflict with other people in the company. These business leaders often receive feedback from colleagues that they have to communicate better and demonstrate they're concerned about the welfare of employees. The resolution of these conflicts frequently involves the business leader sending out a newsletter or using some other medium to prove he's a good guy.

Such resolutions completely miss the boat. For this business leader, the underlying issue is that he's afraid to let his people know him for fear they'll discover he's a fraud. He thinks it's a miracle that he was able to achieve the success he has, and he's convinced that if he drops his aloof fascade people will see through him. Unless someone talks to this business leader and helps him articulate what he's really afraid of, all the communication vehicles in the world won't resolve the conflict between this leader and other employees.

GETTING TO THE ROOTS

How do you unearth underlying issues? Ask these two questions:

- Why does the argument come up when it does?

- How does it leave people feeling?

Unless we answer these questions, we will always deal with symptoms rather than the real cause of conflict. The typical conflict management approach—which we'll talk about in more detail later in this chapter—attempts to change people's behaviors. Bill always disrupts meetings with loaded questions, so we attempt to get Bill to realize that his questions are disruptive and not ask them. Bill's question-asking proclivity, however, is merely a symptom. Underneath those questions, the real issue is that Bill believes that no one cares about him or his ideas. In fact, the lack of acknowledgment of and respect for people's feelings forms the core of every conflict.

Clarifying the discrepancy between surface and underlying issues gets at this core. Management, however, traditionally avoids this clarifying action. It goes back to the thoughts-versus-feelings issue. We're quick to tell our people what to do; we'll suggest a solution to a problem at the drop of a hat. But in our rush to solutions, we ignore feelings, and that's a mistake. Before we decide what to do—how to solve the problem—we need to find out what the underlying issue is. We need to acknowledge the feelings that are at the core of the conflict.

Perhaps the best example of this can be seen when companies make major changes. In some instances, these changes produce many employee protests and complaints—"We're never going to be able to adapt to the new system" or "I don't know why we have to use these new procedures when the old ones worked just fine." When managers hear these complaints, they think they have one purpose: Employees want the changes rescinded and things working like they used to. In reality, the vast majority of employees aren't so naive that they want or expect a return to the good old days. What they do want is for management to acknowledge their feelings. Specifically, they want top executives to admit that they've made their lives more complicated and difficult and stop acting like everyone should be happy with the changes. With that acknowledgment, an organization is on its way to managing a conflict.

STEP TWO: SETTING EXPECTATIONS

The second step in the process is virtually self-explanatory. Setting expectations means communicating what you want to get out of interactions with another person. In most cases, people's expectations are simple and easy to meet. For one person, it may be that he expects to be told he's done a good job when he completes a significant task; he doesn't require any particular reward, just verbal approbation. Set your expectations by communicating what you want people to do when they deal with you.

Some people go around with a black cloud over their heads because they never bothered to set expectations. Though the solution seems obvious, we overlook the obvious when we're frustrated and furious. A common example is a manager who suffers in silence when a colleague constantly hovers over him while he's talking on the phone. The manager wishes his colleague would look in the office, see him on the phone and return later. He finds it infuriating to have his colleague buzzing around him like a persistent fly. Unless he makes his expectation clear to his colleague, however, he'll continue to buzz.

STEP THREE: DEFINING LIMITS AND BOUNDARIES

After expectations are articulated, the next step is for people to state what expectations they can and cannot meet. In other words, they need to set limits on what they're willing and able to do. If someone says, I want you to do A, B and C, we need to respond, I can do A and B, but not C.

The problem occurs because people are reluctant to admit that they can't meet all your needs. We've been raised to believe that if we don't meet every single need, others will want nothing to do with us. It's very difficult for a subordinate to tell his supervisor, I can't meet that expectation. It's difficult because the unstated consequence of not meeting a superior's expectation is termination. In fact, termination occurs when we tell superiors we can meet all their expectations and fail to do so.

From management's perspective, setting limits on expectations involves telling people what management will and will not provide them. When people feel deceived—when they expected x and received y—they find it intolerable. It's far easier for them to live with disappointment than deceit. Most employees can handle disappointment if some of their other needs are being met. It's when management hides information or misleads people that problems occur. For instance, managers allow employees to believe a promotion is forthcoming, when in reality they have no intention of promoting them. Another common deception involves employee benefits— employee healthcare costs go up and management says that the increase is only temporary and they'll try and bring costs down in the future, knowing full well that costs will continue to rise.

STEP FOUR:
TAKING OWNERSHIP OF CHOICES

Given the expectations that have been set and the limits that have been defined, what choices have been created for both people in an interaction? We have to recognize that choices exist and that taking ownership of those choices is crucial.

For instance, in a dispute between a supervisor and a subordinate, the subordinate makes it clear that he will meet some but not all of the supervisor's expectations. The supervisor must then define her choices as a result of the limits placed by the subordinate, and those choices might include the following:

- She can fire her subordinate for insubordination.

- She can reevaluate whether she made a legitimate request.

- She can decide that the other person is quite capable of doing what she requested but that she phrased the request poorly and needs to rephrase it.

- She can determine that the request hit an emotional hot button and that they shouldn't do anything about the request until they talk about the underlying emotional issue—what the subordinate feels about the request, not just what he thinks about it.

The subordinate has corresponding choices. For instance, one choice would be that he decides he can't meet a certain expectation because it conflicts with his values, and the result may be that he has to leave the organization. Another choice may be that he is taking that position because he can't stand the person who issued the request and not because he's incapable of doing it.

The point is that both parties need to say, "These are my choices, and these are your choices; each of us has to choose." They also both need to know the implications of their choices and which ones they want to live with. When this is done, people begin taking ownership of their choices.

At this point in the process, something remarkable happens. People who were locked in intransigent positions suddenly become more flexible. They both had attached themselves to their positions like barnacles, hanging on for dear life. This inflexibility is a result of unexplored feelings. Once those feelings have surfaced, people become much more tolerant and reasonable. Heated conflict simmers down. When they realize how they really feel about the underlying issues, they find choices they can live with. The plight of fired middle managers searching for jobs illustrates this point. During their search, they're sometimes offered entry-level or low-level positions, and they indignantly turn them down, saying that those jobs are demeaning. It's not that they really find such jobs unacceptable; it's that they're terrified of never finding another job again. Once they acknowledge and articulate that fear, they are much more willing to reenter the workforce at any level, including a low one.

STEP FIVE: MAKING A DECISION

You may recall that in Chapter 12, we talked about how expectations without time frames are no expectations at all. The same holds true here. Time frames bring the conflict management process to a close. We need to decide when we're going to act on the choices we've set up. We need to say, "By Monday, we're both going to tell each other what we've decided."

Earlier in this chapter we described the conflict between a veteran sales rep and his new manager. Let's examine how they might manage their conflict productively and reach the fifth step described here.

They begin with an honest talk about how they each see the role of a sales rep. The rep explains that he is accustomed to working in a certain way and was never told that the rules had changed. The manager articulates her expectation that a rep should be spending time laying the groundwork for new levels of corporate partnering, not just taking orders. Underlying issues emerge, such as the rep's dislike of being managed by someone with less experience "in the trenches" than he has. It turns out that the manager felt the rep didn't respect her position, which was why she responded to his attitude by being autocratic.

When these feelings are articulated, the two people begin setting expectations. The sales rep expects respect for his experience and more positive feedback about his excellent sales record. The manager expects respect for her authority and that the rep will work to fit the role she has established for all reps. To define limits and boundaries, she establishes clearer guidelines about how he can use his expense account and how she wants the company represented. He expresses concern that he won't be able to present new technologies without the help of a knowledgeable assistant or some retraining. The sales rep begins to take ownership of his choice to learn his new role. In response, the manager arranges to get him together with the technological development team—he has the option of drawing on the team for assistance, but the presentations will be his show. Relieved that he's still in charge, the rep feels challenged and excited about showing how well he can perform. They set a time frame: He'll get together with the "techies" on Monday and have a presentation ready for the big technology convention next month.

WHAT'S WRONG WITH THE OTHER CONFLICT MANAGEMENT PROCESSES

The five-step process I've outlined here may seem diametrically opposed to the one you're used to. It probably is, because this is a high risk process as opposed to a low risk one. Let's briefly examine the three most common conflict management approaches.

THE BEHAVIOR-ORIENTED MODEL

The premise here is as follows: You tell me what you're going to do, I'll tell you what I'm going to do, and we'll negotiate how much each of us is willing to give up doing. This model is based only on current behaviors that we can identify and stipulate. It's been a very popular approach in recent years, and it works well if you're always dealing with present-day issues. In most instances, however, it ignores underlying issues and concentrates on outward actions. As a result, this approach may create a resolution of a conflict between two reasonable people, but the conflict will emerge in another form because the resolution ignores the real reason for the conflict.

This happens all the time with salespeople who have become nothing more than order-takers. Sales are down, and management has to do something about the situation. So a sales manager cuts an unproductive salesperson's territory in half, but to make that reduction palatable, he gives him a commission bonus. Everyone is happy for the moment, but the real issue has been skirted, and the salesperson will continue to be unproductive.

THE FEELING MODEL

The premise here is that conflicts can be resolved by venting feelings. There's no question that people can feel better when they talk about how they feel. I see companies that encourage employees to come in and talk to management or human resources personnel when they're angry or upset. Employees share their feelings with supervisors and leave the office happy and satisfied. They feel that the company really cares about its employees. But it's only a matter of days or weeks before they require another session to rehash the same issue. These people go from crisis to crisis, becoming addicted to the emotional outpouring that a personal crisis permits. They only feel good when they release the emotional pressure that keeps building up inside of them.

The problem with this approach is that it never addresses the need to change. It doesn't require people to channel their feelings into some practical action. Just as intellect without feelings is a bankrupt approach, so too is feelings without intellect.

THE AUTOCRATIC MODEL

Companies that adopt this model have a parent figure who unilaterally resolves conflicts. It's the ultimate caretaking posture in which everyone opts out of the decision-making process except the wise parent. This parent/boss may make a wise decision that resolves the conflict effectively, but he prevents the people involved from participating in the process. As a result, they never learn to resolve conflicts themselves. Sooner or later, another conflict will arise and they'll go running back to the parent/boss. As the conflicts mount, the parent/boss burns out.

COMMON TYPES OF CONFLICT

An additional problem with the three models just discussed is that they're not well suited to all types of conflict. Conflict can take many forms, and a high risk conflict management strategy encompasses all of them. Let's look at the three most common types and how (and how not) to deal with them.

US VERSUS THEM

First, there is the age-old battle between those who manage and those who are managed. From the worker's perspective, the conflict is, "You don't appreciate my point of view because you don't have to do this stuff." From the manager's perspective, the conflict is, "You don't appreciate my point of view because you don't have bottom-line responsibility for getting it done." This conflict has been with us since the time of robber barons versus unions. Today, the conflict is more sophisticated, often involving a quality-circle group in the factory versus a management team.

No matter how this conflict manifests itself, the "us-versus-them" mentality is a surface issue. The real issue is often the growth and development of the company—or why people at the company aren't growing and developing. This is a tough, complex issue—neither management nor the workers is committed to confronting the barriers to growth and development; they don't want to deal with their mutual decision to choose to stagnate instead of grow. Instead, they generate a pseudo conflict. It's much easier to create an artificial dispute than to admit that the work environment is a "coal mine" for both workers and managers, and they have colluded to keep it that way.

The solution in these conflicts is the first step of our five-step process: clarifying discrepancies—in other words, what the real issue is.

TERRITORIALITY

This is also referred to as the silo mentality. The manager of one division says to the manager of another division, "Don't mess with my area because you don't know what you're doing." It takes place when people from different groups in the company are supposed to work on cross-functional teams, and they can't synchronize their progress; a manager from one group says to another, "We're ready to move, but you guys are holding us back."

Territorial conflicts stem from low-trust postures. They have nothing to do with worries that the other person is incompetent or incapable of understanding. They have everything to do with fears of losing control, a low-trust trait. In many of our companies, managers don't trust anyone or anything outside of their territory— their departments, divisions, or plants. They will find scores of "functional" reasons for not working with others unless this issue is addressed.

Again, the five-step process helps people confront why they have so little trust in others.

PERSONALITY CONFLICTS

The name of this conflict is a misnomer. The more you dig into the alleged personality clashes between any two people who work together, the less you find anything of substance. It's rarely about specific, concrete matters and usually about people's feelings getting hurt. One guy hates another because "he never asked my opinion on any important issue." The conflicts are generally over relatively minor matters, and they get blown way out of proportion. The problem is that the person you're clashing with is a symbol for someone in your past—usually a family member whom you have undealt-with feelings toward.

When I tell managers this, they usually are skeptical. They insist the conflict is because the other person is a jerk and not because of something that occurred in the distant past. I then ask them how long the conflict has been going on. Many respond that they've been feuding for years. I then tell them, "If the issue were related to present behavior, two intelligent people could sit down and work it out. If it has something to do with the past, that's when it becomes irresolvable and begins to feel like a life-or-death issue."

The only way out of these so-called personality conflicts is again by understanding the underlying issue. To unearth it, ask the following questions:

- Why are you so emotionally overwrought with this person?

- In what ways does the other person act toward you that are familiar?

- Let's say this other person always treats you unfairly. Looking back at your past, could you say the same thing about some other person (who often treated you the same way)?

These probing questions often reveal that the antagonistic coworker is remarkably similar to a father, mother, or some other family member with whom a conflict occurred.

Integrating these questions into the five-step process is easy. What's difficult is securing a commitment to the process from the two conflicted individuals. They're reluctant to make commitments because one or both of them are still caught in the underlying issue. Because Jack sees Frank as symbolic of his hateful stepfather, he holds on desperately to his animosity even as he appears to be using the process.

If you have two people in your department engaged in a personality conflict, you need to emphasize that the organization insists on a resolution and won't tolerate this type of unproductive conflict and that if they don't work out their problems, one or both of them will be terminated.

TAILORING THE PROCESS TO PEOPLE AND CIRCUMSTANCE

Before we leave conflict management, I should emphasize that you don't need to use this process for every squabble and disagreement. Minor conflicts generally resolve themselves. The five-step process is designed for major problems, not minor ones.

You will also find a facilitator helpful to start the process and sometimes to see it all the way through. Someone who isn't psychologically triggered by the relevant issues has the objectivity necessary to initiate and hold people accountable for using the process. At some point down the line, people in conflict can often work through the issues on their own. Sometimes, however, a facilitator must be involved from start to finish. When two individuals are carrying heavy emotional baggage—as in the case of personality conflicts—a facilitator is important. Sometimes work conflicts are like a dog fight—you can't stop it unless you give them both solid whacks. A facilitator "whacks" people in conflict by injecting discomfort and accountability, thereby catalyzing changes.

C H A P T E R
ANGER
AND
PRODUCTIVITY

We have seen that bringing a value-based management system into the workplace will generate conflict, and anger often accompanies this conflict. The conflict management process won't work unless people understand and use their anger. When you can't use your anger, the process will fail to resolve conflicts, and you'll be tempted to blame the process for that failure. In this chapter, we'll look at anger—what it is, what it isn't, and how it can be used as a catalyzing force to bring about positive change.

Anger is the most misunderstood emotion in our culture. To resolve conflicts and other personal and professional problems, we need to redefine anger. Contrary to common belief, anger is a normal and healthy response to a difficult situation, and if harnessed can increase professional productivity and personal growth. However, when it is denied and unexpressed, anger becomes transformed into chronic hostility or passivity.

A THIRD MODEL

Most organizations possess either a hostile or a passive culture. In some, tacit approval is given to yelling and screaming. The underlying assumption is that it's healthy for people to engage in shouting match-es—that it clears the air. When a veteran employee lashes out at a junior one, it's considered a rite of passage, similar to the hazings endured by new members of a fraternity. In other organizations, intel-lectual co-opting is the norm. Voices are never raised and no one is reprimanded. The driving force is to keep everyone calm and happy. While this type of culture might look nicer than a hostile one, the anger and disappointment are just as repressed.

In this chapter, I'm suggesting a third model. Rather than occu-py the middle ground between hostility and passivity, I suggest we need to explore new territory: neither the irrational screaming of a hostile culture nor the touchy-feely, emotional cowardice of a passive one. Its basic premise is that expressing anger and disappointment is not only emotionally healthy, but a way to increase productivity.

People feel angry when there's a discrepancy between what they have and what they want. For instance, people are angry when they live in a small house but harbor a vision of their dream house. They can either use that anger to motivate themselves to make their dream come true, or they can let it push them toward passive resignation of their small house fate. Similarly, people become angry when they have no-growth jobs but desire jobs with authority and responsibility. Again, they can use that anger as an incentive to get the job they want or they can resign themselves to their lousy, boring jobs.

Anger is an emotion that expresses and articulates the feeling of disappointment. In fact, disappointment is the primary emotion, and anger the secondary one. Anger is only effectively expressed as disap-pointment. Someone who has difficulty with anger always has difficul-ty with disappointment. A middle manager complains about burning out because he's working excessively long hours, but he never feels his anger or expresses his disappointment in his employees who make chronic mistakes—mistakes that he's working long hours to correct.

The chart on page 197 enables you to to see what happens when you're able to experience anger (as well as what happens when you can't).

HOW ANGER GETS SHUT DOWN

When we don't express our anger or disappointment, it's because someone has shut it down through intimidation or co-opting. Using intimidation, a boss bullies us into "calming down." Using the more

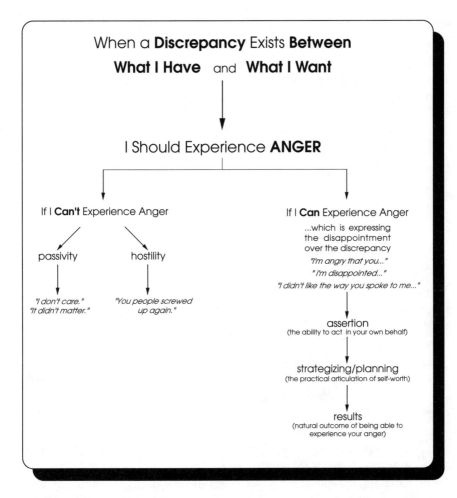

intellectual approach of co-opting, a manager talks us out of being angry and disappointed.

When this happens, our dysfunctional response is passivity or hostility. The passive response is characterized by apathy, disinterest, or sometimes feelings of unworthiness. Typical passive statements include "I don't care" and "It didn't matter anyway." The hostile response is characterized by globalization and personalization. Typical hostile statements include "All you people do everything wrong" and "All of you are totally screwed-up jerks."

Passivity and hostility enable us to deny not only anger and disappointment but the conflict discussed in Chapter 14. The preferable alternative is to experience anger and the four-step process that leads to increased productivity.

THE FOUR-STEP
PROCESS FOR USING ANGER

STEP ONE: EXPERIENCING ANGER

The first step in the process is to express anger. This expression doesn't require foot stomping, shouting, or other forms of hostility. It does require a direct or implied statement of disappointment. For instance, "I'm disappointed that I didn't get the job we talked about." Or, "I don't like the way you spoke to me."

People sometimes assume that they can handle anger if they eliminate any emotion from potentially volatile encounters. Their rationale is that they will maintain a stoic countenance as they express anger and thereby avoid hostility. The problem, however, is not that all emotion should be eliminated; it's that the wrong emotion, hostility, should be eliminated and the right one, disappointment, should be manifested.

Unfortunately, our culture frowns on displays of disappointment. It inculcates the concept that we don't have any right to be disappointed. For instance, a child who expresses disappointment in a drawing he creates at school will prompt a teacher to say, "Oh, don't be disappointed, you did a great job." Lying to children is *not* the way to respond to disappointment.

Companies, too, have a tremendous fear of disappointment and related "down" emotions. The prevailing notion among management is that if people feel disappointed and down, they'll simply give up and never do anything again. A disappointed employee, so the thinking goes, will never marshall the enthusiasm or energy to reach his or her goals. That's demeaning nonsense, of course. People are far more resilient than companies give them credit for. Employees can express this emotion and get on with their lives and jobs. The inability to express it leads to people becoming stuck and fixed in time. Managers who try to prevent their people from feeling down are struggling with the exact same feelings—they want their people to feel "better" so they won't have to deal with their own pain. They're the ones wearing smile buttons and mouthing optimistic aphorisms;

they're so uncomfortable with their own and other people's feelings that they feel compelled to try and change them.

STEP TWO: ASSERTION

People who are able to express their anger as disappointment then move on to the next stage: assertion. *Assertion* means standing up for yourself; acting in your own behalf; affirming yourself; putting yourself forward and seeing to it that your needs are met. It does not mean being difficult, obnoxious, or knocking down anyone who gets in your way. There is nothing hostile about assertion. Hostile individuals so distract others with their abrasiveness that getting their own needs met becomes subordinated to winning power struggles. Hostile employees are a major drag on peak performance. A corporation needs assertive employees, however, because people who can't act on their own behalf won't act on behalf of their companies. Passive, wimpy people don't protect the organization's or their own interests; they're classic fence straddlers who often create their self-righteous victimization.

When we act in our own behalf, we're saying that we value ourselves enough to take care of our own needs. Our anger compels us to initiate action that turns aside disappointment and leads to positive change. When we learn to recognize our anger/disappointment for what it is, we can use it and work with it to our advantage. When we deny it, however, it will turn us into our own worst enemies.

STEP THREE: STRATEGIZING/PLANNING

When you can act on your own behalf, you are then able to strategize and plan. You create a strategy to get your needs met. This third stage is really an articulation of self worth. Because you feel sufficiently worthwhile to act in your own behalf, you're able to translate that feeling into a more concrete plan.

STEP FOUR: RESULTS

When you plan to get something done, you get results. Results are the practical outcome of being able to express your anger. If you're unable to experience your anger, you won't get results. This syllogism explains why hostile or passive people are so unproductive—they're unable to represent productively their own interests and consequently fail to get results.

GETTING SHUT DOWN
IN THE PROCESS

This description of the four-step process may sound easy to implement. But problems often occur somewhere along the way. The most common problem is that people get shut down; they decide not to get angry. As I briefly mentioned earlier, there are two common ways of getting shut down: intimidation and co-opting (hope trips are a third way that I'll focus on later). To avoid getting shut down using this process, you need to know which way your anger was turned off in the past. If you can identify the shutdown mechanism, you can stop it from negatively affecting you again. Let's examine the two shut-down mechanisms so you can identify the one that's affecting you.

INTIMIDATION

Intimidation makes the fear factor so high that people choose not to get angry. When children express disappointment, we often say, "I never want to see that attitude again" or "Wipe that disappointed look off your face." The message is that if you're not happy with what you have, you get verbally (and sometimes physically) spanked. Kids learn to develop a false front and force themselves to accept what they have and feel they have no right to express disappointment.

The same thing happens at work. Managers decide that marginal employees have had difficult experiences and that they (as managers) have no right to be disappointed in their performances. They don't take clear, decisive actions toward these employees because they don't feel they have the right to do so.

In another work situation, an employee decides that he is going to continue to slog through a job that makes him miserable. He determines that if work were meant to be enjoyed, they wouldn't call it work. His thinking goes that he doesn't have any right to be disappointed in a job that is pure drudgery.

Similarly, people settle into unsatisfying marriages, telling themselves this is all they deserve and that they don't have the right to be happy. These people were intimidated long ago. Based on these past experiences, they automatically assume that they'll be attacked for "wanting too much" if they express their disappointment.

CO-OPTING

Intellectual co-opting is even more likely to shut us down than intimidation. We're skilled at talking others out of their feelings, creating arguments that make sense logically but not emotionally. Let's say someone comes in and tells you that she's unhappy that she failed to receive a much sought-after promotion. You respond, "You're upset about that? Look at how well you're doing compared to other people in your MBA class. You've got a salary that's better than most people we know. How can you be unhappy and disappointed?" Logically, such an argument might be valid. It's true that the unpromoted person is better off than most. But being better off than most is no substitute for failing to be where you want to be. If you've lost an arm, it's no great solace to realize that some people are missing both arms. Does anyone really want to believe that because many other people are unsuccessful, you should be satisfied with your limited success?

Once you determine how you were shut down in the past, you're aware of where you're vulnerable. If you were shut down by intimidation, for instance, you'll have tremendous problems with hostile people. Hostile subordinates will run you ragged—you'll be unable to manage them effectively because you're afraid they'll blow up on you. They summon old fears, and as a result they manage and manipulate you.

Highly intelligent, articulate people will prevent you from moving through the four-step process if co-opting has occurred. They're able to talk you out of your feelings. You'll find that it's very difficult to work with these people effectively, because you're unconsciously afraid of how skillfully they prevent you from expressing your feelings.

ANOTHER SHUT-DOWN POSSIBILITY: HOPE TRIPS

You may find that you're unable to experience disappointment at all; that you never get angry because you're never disappointed. You refuse to give up on people no matter what they do, convinced that it's in your power and your responsibility to "fix" them. If that's the case, you're on a hope trip.

We convince ourselves that we haven't done enough, tried hard enough, or been creative enough to enable a subordinate, coworker, or manager to meet our needs. We convince ourselves of these things because of two types of early life experiences.

The first one involves a child who could never please a parent no matter how well he performed. After he plays well in a football game, his father says, "That was a nice run for a short kid." Or the father responds to a straight A report card by asking why he can't do that all the time. When the child becomes a manager, he hires people who are hypercritical of everything he does. If he were a really good boss, they seem to say, he would give them better bonuses, summer hours, or perfect working conditions. No matter how much this manager gives his people, they're never satisfied. He's unable to step back and out of his hope trip and realize that they're never going to tell him what he wants to hear: You're a terrific guy and we really care about you.

The second scenario involves a child whose parent was depressed all the time; no matter what she did or how hard she tried, she couldn't cheer up that parent. As a result, she becomes a manager who won't give up on anyone. She searches for dysfunctional employees and devotes herself to making those employees happier and more productive. She is incapable of facing the fact that most of these people have chosen to be miserable and unproductive; she finds it next to impossible to tell them to change their ways or they'll be terminated.

Here's an exercise that will work for managers who have gone through either scenario. It will help you realize you're on a hope trip and start experiencing the disappointment that leads to anger:

> *Think about an employee with whom you've had significant problems: He's unhappy and always demanding something from you or he has failed almost every assignment you give him. Write down two sets of facts relative to this employee: (1) all the things you've done to help him; (2) his response to your offers of help. You may want to sit down with this person and recite what you've done and then get his response to your efforts. Either way, you're looking to see if his responses indicate that he's taking responsibility for the problems he has or if he's blaming others (offering excuses, saying it's someone else's fault, etc.). If it's the latter, you're on a hope trip and it's time to get off.*

AN ACTION PLAN FOR EXPRESSING ANGER

Although the hope trip exercise is useful for some people, others will require different tools to express their anger effectively. The following steps will facilitate that expression.

Start with this question when you feel your anger beginning to build:

- **What am I disappointed in?**

When people's blood begins to boil, they ask another question instead: Why am I angry? That question simply focuses our attention on what others said or did to make us angry. In some cases, it isn't what they said or did that causes us to be disappointed, but what they didn't say or do. Let's assume you gave someone a research assignment for a speech, and he only completed half of it. You may think that you're angry because you felt like a fool when you gave your inadequately researched presentation. After the talk, you engage in a knock-down, drag-out argument with your subordinate. You tell him you felt like a fool because he didn't do what he should have; he defends himself by saying that you didn't give him enough time to complete the assignment. At the end of the argument, both of you feel righteous about your positions but have solved nothing.

A better way to approach this situation is to figure out what the subordinate did that disappointed you. You may determine that the real hurt is that he let you down after you placed great faith in him. Though you didn't like feeling foolish, the impact of those unpleasant moments was brief. The real disappointment is in his betrayal of your trust. That's what you need to talk to him about. You have to express your disappointment and tell him that it can't happen again.

The second action step is to:

- **Express disappointment directly and let people know they're not fulfilling your expectations.**

General comments such as "you let me down" or indirect statements of anger such as "you screwed me" stop the process of expressing anger dead in its tracks. No one will give you a productive response to general or indirect statements. It's much better to frame your anger in terms of an unmet expectation. That unmet expectation shouldn't be time and event specific—one deadline missed or one uncalled-for remark. It's far more helpful to express disappointment about a pattern you don't want to develop—constantly missing deadlines, for instance. Talking about disappointment in these terms is healthfully assertive—you're acting on your own behalf by insisting on a trusting relationship.

The third action step is to

- **Frame expectations you need met in terms of a relationship**.

Anger builds stronger relationships; it's a relationship-focused emotion. Hostility and passivity, on the other hand, drive people apart. Therefore, clarify what expectations you need met so the relationship possesses a high degree of dependability. Tell people what you need done and ask them to tell you if they can do it. It's much better to deal with the disappointment of someone saying up front that he is unable to complete a task than to find out later he had no intention of doing it. You need to tell the people around you that if this happens, your disappointment will turn into hostility and undermine the relationship. We can best handle disappointment in relationships when it's dealt with directly; if it's not, it becomes hostility and the relationship is in jeopardy.

The strategy and plan you create needs to address this point: mutually agreed on ground rules for getting things done. If the rules are set down and adhered to, both you and the other person achieve the desired results. Your projects are completed to your satisfaction, and the other person feels validated because his expertise and talent were used to meet your expectations.

TRANSLATING ANGER INTO PRODUCTIVITY

Properly expressed anger generates tremendous amounts of productive energy. People who can translate what they feel (anger) into behavior are far more productive than people who waste their energy trying to hide what they feel. Hostility and passivity drain energy away from the tasks at hand; they make you work overtime to keep the real issues hidden.

Most productivity programs that organizations initiate handicap their employees. Although they help people set goals and hold them accountable, they don't allow them to express how they feel—especially if they feel angry and disappointed. These employees may meet their productivity goals, but at an enormous cost. Because their anger has been capped, it implodes—people may get their jobs done, but they burn out. They get sick and they quit in unusually large numbers. High turnover, absenteeism, and high health insurance rates are all symptomatic of this type of company. This is especially true in hostile organizations that mercilessly whip their employees to achieve productivity goals. Although they might meet those goals, they then experience a downturn as their people burn out, and this rollercoaster of gains and losses continues ad infinitum.

Productivity is also damaged in passive organizations. The problem is that these organizations don't want anyone to become angry with people, so everyone passes the buck. If something goes wrong, no one is willing to admit who caused the problem or where it started, making it difficult if not impossible to fix. In passive companies, they nice you to death. Rather than answering your questions directly, they tell you stories to calm you down.

I recently worked with an executive who had just completed a project. I told him that he had done the project well, but I had three problems with it. Before I could say anything else, this executive launched into a convoluted apology, telling me a long and winding story about the genesis of a problem. I held up my hand and said, "Time out. I'm not blaming you. I'm just disappointed in these three things. You did a great job with everything else, and this is not the end of the world." Because of the passive nature of this organization, he was much more interested in stopping me from being angry with him than addressing the issues at hand.

One final point about productivity: It's not just a measure of the outcome, but a measure of the process that was used to achieve the outcome. This distinction is important because when the focus is only the outcome, you lose your people along the way. People are the most expensive component of a company. They're far more expensive to replace than equipment and other hard assets. Productivity experts place too much of an emphasis on the mechanical end of things—the physical act of putting a product together. To achieve maximum productivity, it's just as important for people to be aware of and express the emotions churning inside them. They need to translate all that emotion into productive energy and not misuse it to hold back anger.

C H A P T E R
LOYALTY
IN A
HIGH RISK
CULTURE

16

Company and employee loyalty is one of the hot-button issues of the 1990s. Employees are furious that companies no longer are loyal to them simply because they've been employed for many years. Businesses go into shock when customers sever long-term relationships because they can get a better deal from another supplier. What once seemed like solid supports—I can always make a good living here at the factory; there will always be room for me on the management track; we can depend on 15 percent of gross revenue from the XYZ account—have been pulled out from under them. People feel betrayed, and as a result they are wasting their energy on an issue that will never be settled to their satisfaction. What they want is a return to blind loyalty—but in a high risk culture, blind loyalty is another safety net that is no longer there.

Blind loyalty dictates that I make a commitment to you, you make a commitment to me, and if that commitment lasts for a given period of time, then that commitment is forever. The underlying assumption is that no matter what you or I do to each other, we should honor our commitment. Based on this assumption, companies forgive employees for being dishonest and give them an infinite number of second chances. The blindly loyal organization discovers that a long-time supplier is using deceptive practices yet punishes them with nothing more than a slap on the wrist. In personal relationships, the blindly loyal spouse repeatedly forgives his or her mate for having an affair or for physical abuse. Blindly loyal people or organizations refuse to say "you disappointed me" and back up that statement with negative consequences if they're disappointed again.

Despite these things, many people continue to view loyalty as a symbol of a truly caring relationship. In fact, it's a symbol of a caretaking one. The traditional concept of loyalty means an unquestioning commitment between two parties. Although staying together through thick and thin sounds noble, it becomes ignoble when staying together prevents either party from growing. For instance, employees stay with companies for years, turning their backs on headhunters and refusing to seek other opportunities. They rationalize these decisions by saying, "The company has always been good to me." Somewhere down the road, however, the company may encounter problems and have to layoff many of its employees or even go bankrupt. The company does not give its employees warning about these possibilities, and when layoffs or bankruptcy occurs, the loyal employee cries, "How could you do this to me?"

Unquestioning loyalty really ends up meaning, "I do things for you, so you're indebted to me." There's no accountability in these types of relationships; there's just indebtedness. People don't hold others accountable for growing and becoming better people. The characteristics of a caring for relationship—challenge, confrontation, and conflict management—are absent. Employees who plateau or regress aren't confronted or challenged. In the name of loyalty, we allow them to assume no-growth postures.

TWO TYPES OF LOYALTY

Blind loyalty has no place in a high risk culture that demands peak performance for survival. Although unconditional acceptance sounds admirable, in fact it encourages mediocrity and stagnation. Does this mean, however, that all relationships based on trust must be avoided? Not at all. What it means is that *blind* loyalty must be replaced by *reciprocal* loyalty. Instead of unquestioning commitment, reciprocal loyalty is based on mutual demands for growth in a relationship. If an employee stops growing, his employer's commitment to him should end. If a company stops growing, an employee's commitment to it should end.

If you think about it, you will realize that blind loyalty works against nearly every new paradigm we've discussed in this book. It causes regression to a caretaking mode; it resists change; it allows adequate work instead of demanding peak performance. A relationship based on blind loyalty is a schmoozing relationship, not an intimate one. It doesn't ask for accountability, and it doesn't set goals.

A relationship based on reciprocal loyalty, on the other hand, is dynamic rather than static. The parties in a reciprocal relationship are committed to mutual change, challenge, and growth. Examples of reciprocal loyalty include the following: An employer helps an employee grow into an outstanding manager with a knack for increasing profits. A vendor works with a client to solve a manufacturing problem, leading to lower costs for the client and some innovative and profitable ideas for the vendor. Two companies form an alliance to develop new technologies and market the products based on those technologies. In all of these cases, the relationships have facilitated growth.

Let's look at the two different types of loyalty from a supplier/customer perspective. A supplier has been doing business with a customer for twenty years. The time comes, however, when the supplier has to raise its prices. It explains to the customer that it has been doing a great deal of risk-taking research and development to create better products and services, products and services that will ultimately benefit its customers. Because of this investment, it has to raise prices.

If the customer subscribes to a blind loyalty point of view, it will respond, "We've been giving you business for twenty years, and now you have the nerve to raise your prices on us. That's gratitude for you!"

Contrary to what this customer believes, the supplier is not being disloyal. The supplier is just confronting the company with the reality that it's now more expensive to do business and unless they share in the costs, neither of them will grow. Confronting the customer in this manner is indicative of reciprocal loyalty. At the same time, of course, the customer has every right to question the supplier about the reasons for the price increase. If those reasons aren't satisfactory, the customer needs to terminate the relationship.

DETERMINING YOUR ORGANIZATION'S LOYALTY TYPE

Is your organization blindly loyal or has it adopted the notion of reciprocal loyalty? It's not always easy to answer that question off the top of your head. Loyalty is a highly emotional issue, and it's often difficult to separate the old type of loyalty from the new. To help you do so, answer the following four questions:

1. Does your company focus most of its training and development on new or on veteran employees?

If it's the former, that's a sign of blind loyalty. The organization figures that after it's trained its new people, they will feel that they owe the organization something and remain out of loyalty. Veteran employees feel they can't leave the company because management has made such a sizeable upfront investment in them. The question veteran employees should ask themselves is: When was the last time you attended a meaningful, company-sponsored seminar or other worthwhile training and development session?

2. Do most people in your organization continue to do the same job year after year?

Or are they shifted from job to job and department to department so they can continually face challenges and grow? If not, blind loyalty is operative.

3. Does your company keep people trapped in their roles?

This is a variation on the previous question, in that it suggests that blindly loyal organizations keep people trapped in one role or job to ensure that they can't go anywhere else. When companies don't encourage employees to try new things, they're setting traps for their people and capping the growth of the organization.

4. If your company encourages people to try new things, does it also allow them to return to their old jobs if things don't work out?

A characteristic behavior of a blindly loyal company is to give lip service to growth but provide negative incentives for it. By allowing people to return to their old jobs when a new position doesn't work out, they're encouraging people to take the safe, comfortable path. If reciprocal loyalty exists, they tell people before they embark on a new venture that there's some risk involved; they also warn them that they won't be rewarded with their old position if growth and development don't take place.

MAKING THE TRANSITION

Moving an organization from the old to the new concept of loyalty isn't easy. When blind loyalty has been a part of the culture for years, companies cling to such loyalty like a security blanket. To let go and make the transition to reciprocal loyalty, consider the following two tactics:

- **Change the basis of the organization's compensation system.**

Does your company reward people for just putting in time? Is seniority the best path to promotions, salary increases, and perks? To move away from this blind loyalty reward system, you need to start rewarding people for showing initiative and growth. A performance-based compensation system is the ultimate goal. I've worked with companies who have told their people that they will be frozen at their current compensation levels unless they improve their performance or make new and creative approaches in that direction.

- **Instill the idea that everyone's goal is to challenge and confront the system to make it better for everyone.**

Blind loyalty fosters the idea that people should keep quiet about what's wrong with the organization because criticism implies disloyalty. The key is to model behavior that condones constructive criticism of the system. Not only do you want to encourage objective analysis of weak points and problems, but you want to make sure you don't respond defensively during this analysis. A client of mine recently invited customers to focus-group sessions at which the client told them, "We want to find out what we're doing right and wrong, and we can't do that unless you're honest with us about how we've been serving you. We can't meet your needs unless you feel free to criticize us."

Loyalty used to mean that if you criticized someone, you damaged the relationship. Reciprocal loyalty, however, holds that if you don't criticize a relationship, you're abandoning it. This notion changes the way companies view customers. Rather than being seen simply as someone to serve, customers are now viewed as a resource for growing the company.

THE MOST DIFFICULT OBSTACLE

Many organizations that have made it past the start-up phase and are entering periods of significant growth find loyalty an especially problematic issue. The founders built the company based on everyone's commitment to a vision. Employees banded together and focused on that vision. The commitment people made to each other was strong and necessary for the company to survive those early years. But as the company matures, its relationship with its employees needs to change. Management can no longer make unquestioning commitments to everyone. If it does, employees will stagnate. Management needs to challenge and confront employees to help them grow.

This is difficult for a company's founders. They look at the people who helped them survive some very rough periods and think, "We owe them for their loyalty." But if this sense of indebtedness means allowing them to slide by with mediocre work, they're doing them no favor. In family businesses, I've often had to advise the children and grandchildren who come into the business to confront the founders about this issue. I explain that they need to communicate to their parents or grandparents that what they did was great, but now their notions of blind loyalty are stagnating the company.

Even in larger, older organizations, the notion of indebtedness persists. Major corporations like IBM and General Motors used to protect their people from the outside world. Their enticing recruiting pitch was, "Come work for us and we'll protect you from marketplace and economic vagaries." Years ago, that pitch was valid. If an employee gave GM his unquestioning loyalty, he received a job for life. There was no pressure on that employee to grow and develop. Now, however, any company that offers this same blind loyalty pact is offering nothing. It deludes people into thinking that they don't have to grow, develop, or respond to change. When they are downsized out of jobs, they're unequipped to deal with the fast-moving changes occurring outside their company's walls. Many of these people become the chronically unemployed.

Another way to view this emotional issue involves drawing an analogy between loyalty to one's country and loyalty to one's company. When it comes to one's country, patriotism and free speech are two key principles that immediately come to mind. On the surface, these two principles seem contradictory. Yet we've found that we can be both patriotic and harshly critical of our institutions; that we can believe in our system yet feel free to challenge it. Reciprocal loyalty advocates the same thing: we can remain committed to our people and our company, but we need to challenge and confront them constantly.

PART FIVE
AUTONOMY, STRUCTURE, AND ETHICS

CHAPTER
AUTONOMY AND INDEPENDENCE

17

Do you dream of being the classic entrepreneur, running a business by the seat of your pants and dependent on no one?

Do you manage your company, division, department, or plant your way, refusing to listen to advice and counsel because no one knows how to manage it better than you do?

Are you in or do you want to be in the type of business where you have the capital and market position that insulates you from social, technological, and economic forces that affect others?

If you answered these questions affirmatively, you have a strong independent streak. Although that independence may have been an admirable and quintessential American trait, it has no place in a high risk culture. As people make the transition to the new notion of loyalty described in Chapter 16, they are often surprised to find that their independence is an anachronism. Because loyalty now translates into reciprocal relationships, we can no longer work and live with a stubborn individualism. We can run neither companies nor countries in isolation. Whether we like it or not, an information-intensive culture has forged links between people who had never been in contact before. An Australian ice cream company has to change its entire line of flavors to accommodate a burgeoning market in China (where people didn't like the company's traditional flavors). Computers and other high-speed, high-volume communication vehicles reveal how we're touched by events that occur on the other side of the globe.

Thanks to computer modems, even a small business can stay in touch with and take advantage of shifting economic conditions around the globe. Through Internet™ and commercial online information services, any individual can easily connect with suppliers, shippers, sales agents, and legal and customs experts on any continent. A furniture designer in Texas takes bids from manufacturers from around the world through her computer, keeping her costs low and her prices competitive. A U.S. office supply company found a niche for itself by using a modem to locate products made by Pacific Rim manufacturers to resell in Europe. After the collapse of the Soviet Union, a tiny Florida company that manufactures boating decals used an online information system to contact yacht clubs in the Ukraine.[1]

In a high risk culture, information creates interdependence. To understand how we can adjust to and capitalize on this fact, let's put our interdependence in a human development context.

THE THREE STAGES OF DEVELOPMENT

Psychologists, sociologists, and other observers of human behavior have described human development using a three-stage model. It's a useful model not only for the development of people, but for society and business.

The first stage of human development is *dependence*. In this stage, people feel that they know and can do very little on their own and look to others for direction and guidance. Children obviously feel this way, as do citizens of countries in transition and turmoil—dictatorships arise because people have a need to be told what to do when they feel frightened and unsure.

The second stage is *independence*. Here, the prevailing sentiments are, "I know what to do, I don't need anyone, and I can do it

---

[1] Patricia Haris and David Lyon, "Run for the Borders," *CompuServe Magazine*, October 1993, pp 31-32.

all myself." This stage most clearly manifests itself in adolescence. It is also the stage in which many American organizations have been stuck. They strike the classic American pose of the rugged individualist. Self-sufficient cowboys and do-everything entrepreneurs could thrive in a nonglobal marketplace, but they can't survive in a global one.

The third stage is *interdependence*. People in this stage know the difference between when they need help and when they don't. They recognize that there is too much information and too many growth opportunities to manage on their own. This recognition enables them to seek out others for help, to recognize that they need to be acutely aware of the connections between their activities and those of others. They understand that what happens halfway around the world can affect them. Hawaii's economy, for instance, recently took a nosedive because of Japan's recession.

NO MORE LONE RANGER

Interdependence is not an easy concept for many people to accept. Our country has romanticized the independent outsider. Many managers who work for organizations dream of the day when they can quit, start their own businesses, and "never be dependent on anyone else again." Such a dream, however, bears no relation to current reality. The days of the sole practitioner are gone, whether that practitioner is an entrepreneur, lawyer, doctor, or builder. That doctor is intimately connected to an HMO, PPO, and three hospitals, whereas the builder's business rises or falls based on environmental rulings in Congress that affect the preservation of forests and thus the price of lumber.

All this doesn't mean we must take a step backward in our development and become dependent again. It does mean that we have to give up our independence for autonomy.

CHARACTERISTICS OF AUTONOMY

Unlike independence, autonomy requires accountability and reciprocity. In a reciprocal relationship, there has to be something in it for both parties—independent people who serve only their own needs aren't capable of autonomy. Similarly, autonomy means that we have the discretion to make our own decisions, but that we must make them within a context of accountability to others.

Some people mistakenly believe they can escape autonomy. If they have enough money or if they quit their jobs and start their own businesses, they assume they don't need other people to succeed. Yet without reciprocal, accountable relationships, they won't make much progress in their careers or their lives. The independent-minded entrepreneur may possess great drive, ideas, and capital when he starts his business, and at first everything will go very well. It's only when he tries to grow his business that he runs into a roadblock. Unless he's able to form reciprocal, accountable relationships with others, he'll lack the resources necessary to move his business forward. In an interdependent, information-driven culture, there's only so much one person can do.

Large organizations are gradually recognizing that they need to shift from independent to autonomous models. Because they require computer technology to manage huge amounts of information, they're becoming acutely aware of how information affects them. For example, working with that technology, they discover forces in another corner of the world that will have a tremendous impact on their industry. It becomes clear that no matter what market they're in or where they're located, there are numerous de facto global connections. To remain independent in the face of these connections is suicidal. The reality of interdependence is driven home when people attend international conferences. Increasingly, the issues that concern attendees from the United States, France, Saudi Arabia, and Australia are the same. In fact, at one recent conference I attended, a business owner from Mozambique was explaining how changes in American buying habits were dramatically affecting his company.

This interdependence exists within organizations as well as on a global level. Yet many companies, divisions, plants, and departments are still run as fiefdoms—as independent rather than autonomous groups. Part of the problem is that they've historically been reinforced for running this way. Management used to reward people who operated their groups with a silo mentality, responding to those who disagreed with the department head's methods by saying, "Don't tell him what to do, he really knows how to run his business." Total quality management has pointed up the flawed reasoning of that response. The cross-functional emphasis of TQM is designed to facilitate sharing of information and an autonomous mindset.

USING HIGH RISK TOOLS
TO BECOME AUTONOMOUS

Many of the high risk skills I've discussed throughout this book are applicable here. For instance, relationship-building skills are critical for autonomy. In an interdependent world, people who are loners or just plain weird and can't deal with others will have a rough time. Those who are able to build reciprocal relationships, on the other hand, will flourish.

The grieving process also proves useful. Many successful businesspeople have built their identity (and the identities of their organizations) around the concept of independence. They will need to grieve the loss of this identity—no longer can they take pride in being the renegades of the industry, viewing everyone else as the enemy. An autonomous organization will have to work with companies that were formerly viewed as enemies.

Values, too, play an important role. In the interdependent stage, partnering is essential. Individuals, divisions, and companies need to work together and exchange resources. Values play a critical role in helping you choose the right partner. If you choose someone whose values are different from yours, the relationship will be dependent or combative rather than interdependent. Value matches ensure parity in relationships and enable both parties to function autonomously.

THE THEORY OF PLENTY
VERSUS THE THEORY OF SCARCITY

Besides these skills, people in an interdependent culture need to believe in the theory of plenty in order to prosper. Unfortunately, the independent-minded theory of scarcity has been drummed into our heads.

This theory teaches that resources are scarce and that cutthroat competition is the only way to get your piece of the pie. The underlying premise is that there's a ceiling on how much market share you can acquire, and that if you don't fight tooth and nail against competitors, you'll get less than your fair share. The theory of scarcity traps its adherents in a survival mode.

The theory of plenty, on the other hand, assumes that infinite resources exist to meet your personal and work needs. Its premise is that no market—nor your share of it—is fixed and finite. Instead, it's continually expanding as you exchange information and resources with people. The more you learn about a market, the easier it is to find ways to grow it. Information and increased competition "legitimize" products and services.

For instance, the worst thing for a therapist's business is to be the only therapist in town. Although that therapist might have a monopoly on the market, it's a very small market. When there's only one therapist, therapy is viewed as something odd and different. If there are more therapists, therapy doesn't have a freak-show aspect. Numerous practitioners have a legitimizing effect; the simple fact that there are many therapists suggests that they have something worthwhile to sell.

This theory of plenty has a profound effect on the way we view competition. Instead of being a threat, competition becomes a resource. It may be that you have to work with your competitors and exchange information with them to grow your market. It may be that you'll need to use some of your competitor's expertise (that you don't possess) to handle a given project. There's nothing wrong with this if you accept that there's plenty of pie to go around. If, on the other hand, you believe you and your competitors are fighting over one small piece, this new competitive perspective will scare you, and you'll dismiss it as a nice theory but impossible to put into practice.

COMPETITION AS A TOOL

It's not that competition ceases to exist in an interdependent world; it's that it exists in a different form. Competition in this world becomes a growth and development tool. It helps all competitors refine what's unique about their products and services and find a niche in a market where the differences between competitors are clear. This is opposed to the old view of competition as a weapon— something to use to eliminate competitors before they eliminate you. You'll remember that we discussed this new view of competitive advantage back in Chapter 3.

A theory-of-plenty frame of reference enables organizations to grow markets that seemed saturated. For instance, the cellular phone market appeared initially to most observers to be a limited growth market. In 1983 when the prediction was that there would be 700,000 users in 1993, insufficient competition existed to push people to explore the technology's range of uses. The creative forces contained in emerging competition, however, drove the marketplace to its current size of 14 million users. For years, companies persisted in the belief that the sole purpose of cellular phones was to keep business-people in touch with their offices. But after a few years of competition, companies began to realize that they'd just barely tapped potential uses—that people would buy cellular phones for everything from use in highway emergencies to keeping in touch with friends. The same type of thinking has turned the telephone from a simple communication device to one that will soon be capable of delivering 500 cable channels to our homes.

Cross-fertilization of ideas is the hallmark of an interdependent culture. The Japanese are very good at this; competitors frequently exchange information to create new markets and expand old ones. American companies still tend to focus on building better mouse-traps and jealously guarding their information.

This fierce independence is representative of a caretaking mentality. It seeks to establish one-way relationships in which one party remains smugly assured that it knows what is best for the other party. Interdependence, on the other hand, reflects a caring for mindset. A number of industries have begun to recognize this, one of which is the insurance industry. Competing insurance companies regularly exchange information. They've also greatly increased the number of focus groups they conduct, sitting down with policyholders to find out how they perceive the company's products and services. Some of the answers to those questions led a number of insurance companies to discover that people who bought policies from them hadn't heard from their agent for as many as three years after the purchase. That astonished company executives, and the more they learned, the easier it was for them to decide what needed attention and changing and what the real marketing problem was as opposed to what it appeared to be.

The increased use of focus groups suggests that more companies recognize that they're in an interdependent relationship with the people they call customers.

HOW TO FOSTER AUTONOMOUS BEHAVIOR

Asking the following two questions when decisions are made in your organization will foster autonomous and discourage independent behavior:

- Who does this decision affect?

- How does it affect them?

In independent organizations, decision-making's sole objective is to get things done. In interdependent organizations, an equally important objective is to connect people. The preceding two questions are designed to facilitate an exchange of information about crucial decisions, to get a network of people talking to and recognizing each other's interests.

Along these same lines, ask the following postdecision question:

- Is it clear to everyone who's accountable to whom for communicating results of decision-making?

Many organizations limit accountability to production of goods and services—people are accountable only for getting a product manufactured or a service delivered. No one, however, transmits information to colleagues affected by the decision, keeping them in the dark about what was accomplished. When people are isolated from key information, an independent system is maintained. Only when people are connected does interdependence flourish.

Two exercises will help you foster the necessary autonomous behavior:

1. After you (or your people) make a decision, make yourself accountable for informing five other people who are affected by that decision.
2. Create a new organizational chart with an interdependent rather than an independent slant. From the previous questions, you should know who is affected by your decisions. This chart reflects all the people affected by all the decision makers. It enables you to foster interconnectedness and avoid leaving people out of the loop.

One of the most common mistakes of independence occurs when individuals or organizations launch new ventures. They focus all their energy and attention on a great idea, on a product or service, or on working night and day to make the venture successful. What they neglect are the human relationships necessary for success in an interdependent culture. They try to do it alone (either literally by themselves or with a relatively small group) and ignore the many people who have the skills and knowledge the venture requires.

For instance, fax machine technology has existed for forty years. It only became a hugely successful product, however, when people pooled their resources. Professionals from the telecommunications, copier, express mail, and consumer electronics industries got together and recognized that a niche in the information delivery market was going unfilled—people didn't want to wait five days for a package of information. What if they could get it instantly with one phone call?

Autonomous people try to bring together the most diverse group of resources possible. Instead of just working with one source like an outside consultant, they gather advice and information from competitors, employees, and suppliers.

If you're considering starting a new business or launching a new product line, take the following two steps:

1. Gather together people with the range of practical and intellectual resources necessary to grow and develop your venture.
2. Evaluate the people you choose not only on what they bring to the table, but on whether they share your values and vision and are willing to communicate them to others.

As difficult as it might be for the more independent-minded people among us to embrace these suggestions, it's absolutely essential. It's important to realize that an interdependent world isn't one that deprives us of our individualism. Instead, that individualism truly prospers within the context of reciprocal and accountable relationships.

CHAPTER

CONTROL, STRUCTURE— AND CONFLICT

18

In an interdependent world, we need structure more than ever before. Without structure, it's impossible for autonomous individuals and companies to work interdependently with other individuals and companies. We require organizational hierarchies to keep our burgeoning people networks functioning efficiently and effectively. We need rules and policies to provide a framework for growth and development.

Members of a trapeze act must be able to depend on the other performers to fill their assigned roles; before letting go of the trapeze to execute a death-defying flip, a performer trusts that someone will catch her before she falls. In the same way, working interdependently in a high risk culture requires depending on others to perform their assigned part of the "act." If we can't depend on others, we soon fall back into a caretaking mode: A few highly committed employees become overloaded, and no one else assumes responsibility. Peak performance is only possible when everyone can be depended on to play his part, to work within the structure.

Despite this, people persist in fighting against structure. They do so because they confuse structure with control. Something occurred in their early family life that transformed them into control freaks. If you are fighting against structure and fighting for control, you'll find it impossible to apply the high risk skills discussed in this book to your work and life. At the same time, if you are managing such people, productivity will suffer unless you can persuade them to give up control for the sake of the company's (and their own) goals.

To help you work through common structure versus control issues, let's begin by defining our terms.

WHAT YOU HAVE TO DO
VERSUS HOW YOU HAVE TO FEEL

Structure simply means that you need to exhibit specific behaviors in order to receive specific payoffs. If you want to reach the top of a company or profession, you have to adhere to the formal and informal policies and performance standards of that company or profession. All structure does is provide a framework for people to grow and develop. This structure is mirrored in normal human development: Children learn that if they take certain actions, they will receive certain rewards. Without the incentive to grow and develop that structure provides, children would never learn anything.

Control also involves exhibiting specific behaviors in order to gain specific payoffs. But it adds one element to that definition: *Control dictates that people have to feel certain ways about their behaviors.* That element produces three counterproductive and highly destructive reactions in people—rebellion, revenge, and power struggles—reactions provoked, for example, by very controlling managers. Managerial insistence on consensus decision-making communicates that all employees should be happy about decisions made (even if they're really unhappy). Management declares that the company will be reorganized and tries to persuade everyone that they should feel good about a decision that may mean months of disorganization and confusion. By trying to take away people's right to feel disappointed, managers create resentful subordinates who eventually will express their resentment in some form of sabotage.

People in companies frequently misperceive the intent of structure. Rather than viewing an assignment from a superior as the company telling them what they need to do, they misperceive it to be the company telling them how to feel about what they have to do. They respond to this misperception by thinking or saying, "No one here is going to tell me what to do." It's at this point that managers should say, "Of course we're going to tell you what to do, but we have no intention of telling you how to feel about it. Don't turn this into a power struggle over control because you have a problem with structure in your life." When managers don't provide their people with this response (and they usually don't), employees become hostile. The source of their hostility isn't found in what's just taken place, but within themselves. To deal with that hostility, managers need to confront their people with a critical choice: Work on your control and structure problem or keep up pointless power struggles and put your future in jeopardy.

WHERE THE CONTROLLING IMPULSE COMES FROM

To get a sense of how and why people reproduce control problems in organizations, let's look at a typical precipitating event from family life. When Jimmy is a boy, his dad tells him to take out the garbage every Tuesday. Jimmy says something like, "I don't want to" or "I'll take it out next week." His controlling father responds, "If you don't take it out now, you'll really be in trouble and you're going to be punished because I don't like your attitude." Jimmy is taught that the problem isn't his behavior but his attitude; in other words, his feelings.

Repeated events such as these lodge in a corner of Jimmy's brain. As a child, he doesn't have the understanding to tell himself that his father is really trying to control his feelings. All he knows is that it makes him mad, and subconsciously he vows, "No one is ever going to tell me what to do again"—not how to feel, but what to do. Years later when Jimmy is a salesperson and his sales manager says that he has to fill out activity reports and must meet a sales quota, Jimmy's reflexive response is, "No one tells me what to do."

Contrast Jimmy's father's response to a parent who understands the importance of structure. When his son tells him he doesn't want to take out the garbage because the job sucks, he would respond, "Of course it sucks. You don't have to like taking out the garbage, you just need to do it."

IDENTIFYING AND RESOLVING CONTROL ISSUES

If you're wondering whether you (or your people) might be operating under the influence of a controlling parent, try the following exercise:

- Think about incidents from your childhood when your parents told you to do something you didn't want to do. Did they permit you to express your feelings or did they try to control those feelings by saying such things as, "Wipe that smirk off your face" or "I don't like your attitude"?

You can observe the impact of such incidents on people within your own organization. Some employees who are embroiled in control battles and power struggles will quit or be fired. Still others will recognize the problem on their own as they become more ambitious: they realize that their hang-up with control is holding them back, and they make a successful effort to rid themselves of this self-destructive behavior.

Some people, however, have no idea what they're doing. You can identify these people by looking for the following two traits:

- They say something to this effect: "Why are people doing these things to me?" and generally act choiceless and powerless.

- They constantly provoke and incite others during interactions.

The former trait suggests people who feel that they have no choice about the structure they're in; it's a fatalistic and passive stance. The key issue is their inability to experience disappointment and their own anger. Instead of feeling justified in being angry and doing something about it, they choose passivity and victimization.

The latter trait is indicative of someone who isn't happy unless he's involved in a hostile and antagonistic relationship. He takes a perverse pleasure in the arguments that come with power struggles. As we discussed in Chapter 15, this is the hostile side of an inability to experience anger and disappointment.

If you're managing this type of person, you need to sit down and confront him by saying something like the following:

Do you find yourself going into interactions at work knowing you're going to provoke and incite others, but you're unable to stop yourself from doing so? Regardless of your best intentions, do you feel trapped, controlled, and that the only way out seems to be to provoke a fight in which you end up being the loser? Then you have to get help, because you're never going to grow and develop if you're always losing power struggles.

DEALING WITH EMPLOYEES WHO CAN'T DEAL WITH STRUCTURE

If you have subordinates who by word or deed indicate that they don't want to be told what to do, pose this question to them:

- Do you want to make a commitment to growth and success in your life, or would you rather engage in a power struggle with me about your unresolved issues?

If the former, you can work with that employee and help him identify what assistance would be useful to him in working through his unresolved issues. If the latter, then that person has no place in a high risk organization.

Another critical guideline to follow when dealing with this type of employee is the following:

- Don't cut people any slack if they habitually fall just a little bit short.

People will test your ability to maintain structure. For instance, you give a salesperson a quota and she falls a few orders short. Or you ask someone to prepare a report by a certain deadline and he delivers it one day late. Your impulse may be to forgive these shortcomings; you feel that you should give them a break or that you don't want to deal with the aggravation that a confrontation would produce.

The problem is that you're being tested, and if you give in you fail the test. By maintaining an unequivocal position regarding expectations and deadlines, you avoid structure-destroying power struggles.

To keep people's focus on structure rather than on control, management needs to use caring for tools such as confrontation, conflict, and challenge. Caretaking responses such as commonality, conflict avoidance, and consensus are attempts to control the way people feel and invariably lead to rebellion and sabotage. In caretaking companies, employees rebel against deadlines by saying under their breath that "the deadline is dumb, so I'm not going to pay any attention to it." Their self-righteous indignation over being told what to do and when to do it is so great that they're even willing to be fired. Control issues set up win-lose situations, and the person without the power always loses. Similarly, control freaks in their intimate relationships will often choose to win a power struggle and lose the relationship; they don't want to deal with an issue raised by their partner that they know in their gut is solid and legitimate.

In caring for cultures, management encourages people to say up front if a deadline is dumb. The opportunity to express how one feels about what one has to do removes most or all of the resistance to doing it. People can deal with disappointment; they can't and won't deal with their feelings being denied.

THE COMMON CONTROL ISSUES

You can avoid many counterproductive control battles by being aware of the four issues over which they most often arise:

- **Deadlines.** People don't like deadlines; they don't like to have to work on weekends or late at night. But people don't always have to like what they do; they need to decide that it's worth doing. There's an old saying in sales: Successful people do what unsuccessful people choose not to do. People need to understand that as onerous as deadlines might be, they have to be met and successful people meet them. A whole lot of time devoted to whining and arguing about deadlines could be allocated to activities that would help people meet their deadlines.

- **Interpersonal relationships.** Personality conflicts occur because one person (or both) in a relationship is trying to control the other. Instead of getting the real structure issues on the table, they become entangled in a power struggle over who's in charge and who's going to get his or her way. These power struggles aren't over substantive matters but over controlling how the other party feels about those matters. Personality conflicts between administrative managers and clerical staff often reach a crescendo of passive-aggressive hostility over who's responsible for cleaning up an area of the office. Clerical staff with control problems want to translate this into a human rights issue, whereas administrative managers perform a ballet of indirectness trying to avoid ordering staff to clean up.

- **Money**. Money is often a real symbol of control. Most managers have been involved in power struggles over salary increases with their subordinates, revolving around employees' statements that "you're not paying me what I'm worth." Whether or not the case is legitimate, most people are really enraged by the fact that they'll have to accept the current structure's limits or find a new job if they have to make more money. People need to realize they'll make more money as a marketing director, salesperson, or commodities trader rather than as a secretary, teacher, or human resources director. These differences are dictated by current structures in the culture. Employees don't have to like these structures, but they do need to make some choices and decisions about them. These choices and decisions are what they control. Contrary to some people's complaints, managers don't control them with money; managers simply tell them what the job is worth, and employees make choices about accepting or not accepting that statement of worth. Money is always a volatile issue because it's one of the key representations of self-worth.

- **Promotions.** "I'm frozen in this job; the company controls my advancement." If you're familiar with this complaint, you've seen a control battle flare over this issue. In reality, the company doesn't control anything—every employee is a free agent, capable of either leaving the organization or staying there and finding a way to advance. It goes back to the notion of risk: People who are risk takers don't have to get in power struggles over these issues; they just need to make decisions and be prepared to deal with the consequences.

A NATURAL STRUCTURE

There's one last argument you may encounter from people who are fighting control battles. They'll tell you that you're trying to impose an artificial structure on them, and that structure isn't natural.

The corporate model that I discussed in Chapter 7—a structure that calls for accountability, delegation, and reciprocity—is a perfectly natural structure. Children would never survive their play experiences without this type of structure—it tells them they can play at the park but not on the highway. Structure teaches them skills such as reading and writing; most kids wouldn't sit down and read a difficult or boring book about grammar on their own. Children don't have to like structure or structure-imposing entities (like the educational system); they just have to do what it requires.

When put in these terms, most people recognize that structure isn't artificial but a natural part of human society and development.

C H A P T E R

DOING
THE
RIGHT THING

19

This final chapter revolves around a question that everyone is asking these days. It's a question that comes up when people are considering such issues as downsizing, mergers, advertising, corporate policies, and supplier relationships:

- What's the right thing to do?

Unfortunately, it's a question that everyone answers differently. Morality is culturally determined, so what's right to one group is wrong to another. Healthy competition in one country is ruthless domination in another. Not only will you find diverse interpretations of morality among countries, but also among companies and departments within companies. One department head thinks it's only fair that everyone on a team receives the same bonus, whereas another department head believes bonuses should be tied solely to individual performance.

Before the global marketplace became a reality, a variety of moral perspectives could coexist. In an interdependent world, however, these varying perspectives cause chaos. Conflicting ethical systems make it impossible for individuals, groups, and countries to work together.

A well-known example of this ethical conflict is the controversy surrounding the exportation of rice to Japan. A Louisiana rice grower might be able to sell high-quality rice to Japan at a lower price than Japanese rice, which would benefit the Japanese consumer. However, Japan severely restricts rice importation to protect the traditional rice farmer, important to Japan's cultural heritage.

The solution is a new definition of ethics, one that is universally accepted. I believe that ethics are beliefs and practices that promote growth, development, and learning. Anything that doesn't promote these things is unethical. That definition should be familiar to you, given the content of this book. Throughout these pages, I've provided you with beliefs and practices that promote growth, development, and learning. Perhaps the best way to illustrate how all this constitutes a new code of ethics is through the chart on the next page.

Let's start at the top of the chart and work our way down. Everything begins with information. Information creates two things: a rapid rate of change and interdependence. Change and interdependence, in turn, create a high risk culture—a culture characterized by unpredictability, uncertainty, and vulnerability.

In this culture, our old notion of security is obsolete. When nothing is predictable, the traditional external symbols of security such as where you live and work, are no longer viable—our jobs may call for us to travel half the year or relocate every few years. The new notion of security is internal and portable, formed and shaped by our core values. They travel with us wherever we go.

When our sense of security is internal instead of external, the focus shifts to growth and development. Such things as living in the same town all your life or working for the same company for thirty years no longer make sense. Instead, it's what you bring to the table right here and now that counts—how you grow and develop. If you stop growing and developing in an information-intensive culture, you'll feel that you're being left behind. Growth and development allow you to keep pace.

As you grow and develop, you are constantly changing; the people around you are also changing. As a result, you'll need to confront and grieve. Confrontation involves dealing with people

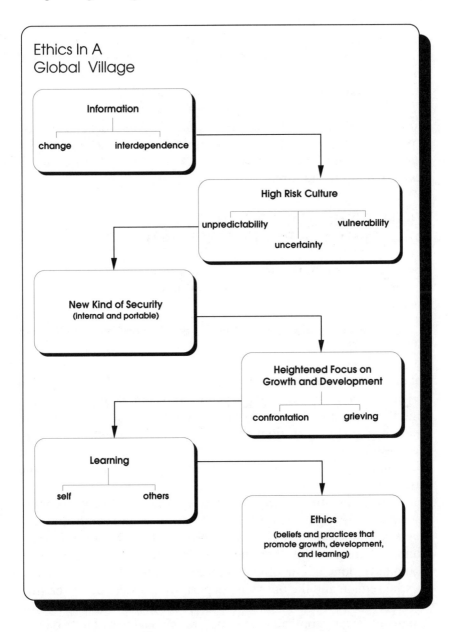

Ethics In A Global Village

Information — change, interdependence

High Risk Culture — unpredictability, uncertainty, vulnerability

New Kind of Security (internal and portable)

Heightened Focus on Growth and Development — confrontation, grieving

Learning — self, others

Ethics (beliefs and practices that promote growth, development, and learning)

who don't do what you expect—the person who Bill used to be would have done A, but because Bill has changed, he now does B, and you have to confront him and yourself about this fact. Grieving is crucial because growth and development produce change and loss. Grieving allows you to deal with these losses—you're not the same person you used to be, others are not the same, the culture is not the same. Grieving helps you let go and move on.

Confrontations and grieving enable you to learn about yourself and others. This learning process is constant and ongoing, part and parcel of our growth and development. Anything that we do to promote this learning process is ethical. Anything that doesn't promote it is unethical—not because it's "immoral," but because it sets people up for failure.

HOW THIS DEFINITION OF ETHICS APPLIES TO YOU

Now that I've traced the linkages from information to ethics, let me answer the questions and concerns that may be occurring to you at this point.

First, isn't the old notion of ethics much more humanistic than this one?

Not at all. It's the old caretaking mentality that's highly immoral. On the surface, of course, caretaking people and companies seem beneficent; they appear to take care of their people in good times and bad. What they really were doing was deluding the people they were allegedly caring for. They made them think they were making a contribution or were doing fine when they were actually stagnant and plateaued.

Caretaking attitudes are exposed for what they really are when you examine them in the wake of downsizing. Many companies that have streamlined their staffs have done so initially because of direct economic pressures, but then they recognize that it's something they should have done a long time ago that will benefit both the employees who remain and the ones who depart. In the wake of downsizing, most management is becoming aware that it's getting more done with 20 percent fewer people than ever before. Managers will tell you that most of the people they let go were terribly unhappy no matter what they were paid; that they were just putting in time. Organizations are now asking themselves a question they never asked in the old caretaking days: Are our people doing meaningful work that keeps them marketable and employable and keeps them growing and developing? If the answer is no, it's unethical to delude them and allow them to remain with the organization.

Another common concern is,

Given my job or business, are ethics really relevant?

I recently gave a talk about ethics after which a member of the audience said, "All this is interesting, but I'm in a business that makes poorly made products that we sell at overinflated prices in underdeveloped countries, and we usually have to bribe one official or another to keep things running smoothly. I don't do anything to promote growth and development. Are you telling me I ought to give this up?"

That's exactly what I told him. I explained that sooner rather than later, underdeveloped countries will become more developed and no longer tolerate his company's practices. Even worse, his unethical attitude represented a very limited vision of what he could do with his business and his life and what his employees could do with their lives. Not only will the developing country exact revenge at its first opportunity; the employees of this low-ethics operation will find themselves unemployable when the company goes under.

Caretaking, unethical attitudes diminish people's capacities for productivity, achievement, and quality of life. These attitudes lead to limited views of people's abilities and options and often create unintended incentives for destructive or criminal behaviors.

This brings us to a third frequently voiced concern: Isn't the ethical construct you present a prescription for a cruel, Darwinian world?

Again, the problem is one of perception rather than reality. We've been taught that the old caretaking, low risk model is good for us. But what is crueler: to allow people to be miserable, unproductive, and temporarily employed or to alert people that they've plateaued and that if they don't start growing and developing, they won't have a job?

My definition of ethics fits a high risk culture. In this culture, numerous growth opportunities exist for everyone. People can achieve far more than they've ever achieved before, and they shouldn't sell themselves short. Ethical behavior enhances people's capacities and literally opens the world to them. Ethics enable them to take advantage of all the growth and development opportunities available in this culture.

Ethics are good for individuals, and they're good for the companies they work for, own, and manage. People who are growing and developing are far more productive than those who are stagnant.

Throughout these pages, I've provided you with tools and techniques that will help you and your people grow and develop. These tools and techniques won't be effective, however, unless viewed and used within the context of a high risk culture. I've attempted to explain what that culture is and how to live and work productively in it.

That culture is neither Darwinian nor Orwellian. It is a highly ethical culture, unlike the low risk culture of the past. Then, companies could prosper even though they didn't promote individual growth and development; they could rule their organizations like benevolent despots, treating their people kindly but never caring a whit about helping them learn new skills or find new challenges. As long as the employees did their jobs, it didn't matter if they were bored and mindlessly repeating the same tasks day after day.

In today's environment, such an attitude is unethical. It is also a prescription for individual and organizational failure.

CONCLUSION

At the beginning of this book we discussed the crippling effects of denial on American business. We have also discussed the importance of the caring for paradigm in our personal and professional lives.

When we put these two elements together, we see that part of caring for ourselves is not allowing ourselves to be stuck in denial. As individuals we must learn to tell ourselves what we need to know—what is real—and not what we want to believe. Self-honesty is a component of growing into adulthood. We can be guided in this process by a firm set of values, while we allow ethics to shape our actions and decisions. Meeting the challenge of the high risk culture begins with each of us.

These are frightening and chaotic times. However, I believe that by the use of the skills and practices presented in this book, we can create a strong economy, a stable society, and productive, satisfying personal lives.

ACKNOWLEDGMENTS

The foundation for the writing of this book was built by a number of life-shaping and life-changing experiences, as well as the support of several individuals who had strong beliefs in themselves and in me.

The family and subculture I grew up in placed a high value on knowledge, learning, and teaching. As early as I can remember, I was exposed to a constant stream of information and a large variety of differing people and environments. My grandmother, Sarah, was a current events hound and she held us accountable (sometimes on a daily basis) for knowing what was going on in the world. I have often described (only half-jokingly) that dinner time, during my childhood and adolescence, was very much like being interviewed on "Meet the Press." My mother, during those years, encouraged us to meet and welcome into our home schoolmates and other friends from a wide variety of backgrounds and experiences. And the extensive travel, throughout the world, that she and my father loved so much modeled the coming globalism that has become an integral part of my life and that of our children.

The year I spent in England in the 1960s', as a student at Leeds University, was truly a life-changing experience. Those were still the days when the political, economic, and intellectual elite of the world sent their young adults to English universities to be educated and acculturated. Sixty-five countries were represented in my dorm, and almost thirty on my floor alone. Dinner every night was like a session at the United Nations, except that we had representation from countries (like Red China) that were excluded from the UN. I was at Leeds during the Cuban Missile Crisis, and my experience of that watershed event in world history was radically different from that of most Americans, and had a profound affect on me.

My two experiences in psychotherapy were both life-altering. The first was in psychoanalytic therapy, and the exposure it gave me to psychoanalysis and Freudian thought has proven, to this day, to be the quintessential educational experience of my life. It is rare for a day to go by in which I don't use that knowledge base to illustrate the connection between a current decision or behavior and its roots in a client's early past. It is like clearing a fog or lifting a veil of secrecy, and I am continually amazed and impressed by the power of these connections to begin the process of change in individuals who know something is amiss but cannot quite put their finger on it. My only sadness in this area is that psychoanalysis and Freudian thinking are still so poorly and simplistically understood by most people who use concepts derived from them.

As powerful and influential as psychoanalytic therapy was, it paled in comparison to primal therapy as a change agent in my life. From a therapeutic perspective, the psychoanalytic experience made where I had come from and the forces that shaped me exceedingly clear. But from a change perspective, it only succeeded in making me glib and more articulate about my neurotic behaviors. Primal therapy made the feelings about those early shaping forces painfully evident and provided the tools for implementing significant growth and development. The two pieces together – the cognitive framework provided by psychoanalysis and the emotional energy and freedom provided by primal – created the life skills base that allowed me to understand what was happening within and around me and gave me the resources to confront the tough and wrenching issues in my life.

A number of individuals have played key roles in supporting my professional (and personal) growth and development and, in particular, in articulation and concretization of high risk theory and practice. The first of these were Rick Pfeiffer and Don D'Amico. Rick was director of special education at the Mid-Valley Special Education Co-op in St. Charles, Illinois and Don was superintendent of schools in St. Charles. Rick took a lot of risk in bringing me and my confrontive style into public education, and Don took the risk of backing him up. I am grateful to both for their belief in me. We got a lot done for handicapped and troubled kids and took on slews of difficult parents, arrogant mental health professionals, and rigid, mind-numbing educators. We took no prisoners, and we had a great and gratifying time.

After my stint in public education, I was exposed to the law enforcement community in America through Don Thomas, a police officer I had met when we were both members of a drug abuse task force in our local community. Don, who is a friend to this day and director of training at the St. Charles Police Department, introduced me to Pat O'Shea, who, at the time, was the director of the Northeast Multi-Regional Training Center in Aurora, Illinois. Northeast provided training and development for a large Chicago-area consortium of police departments and law enforcement agencies and provided me an invaluable opportunity to solidify high risk concepts as well as to hone my skills as a trainer and presenter. I learned through my four years of law enforcement consulting that if I could deal effectively with difficult and resistant cops, I could deal with anybody.

I really enjoyed working with police officers, and I grew to respect and value law enforcement and the absolutely essential role it plays in maintaining sanity and quality of life in a free and open society. One of my few fears about our future is that we will fail to support law enforcement effectively or, even worse, make it the scapegoat for our inability to confront and set limits on the marginal and criminal population that has plagued our urban and suburban environments.

One last word about this stage of my life. Pat O'Shea is the most dedicated professional I have ever worked with. Pat had been an old-time street cop and had seen things that most of us will never and would never want to see. Instead of turning him bitter and cynical, his experiences created a stronger commitment to professionalizing police work and truly helping officers grow. Pat loves cops. He is one of the most caring men and human beings I have ever known. Through Pat I met Brad Weigel, who is director of training for the Glenview, Illinois Police Department. Brad is one of the brightest, most astute and effective individuals in contemporary law enforcement. Dialoguing with Brad is an experience in intellectual clarity, and watching him work with others gives true meaning to the concept of accountability.

My introduction to business consulting came through Harry Hoopis, the general agent for Northwestern Mutual Life in Northfield, Illinois. Harry built and still manages one of the flagship insurance operations in all of North America. He has combined street savvy, conceptual brilliance, and a drive to achieve to become one of the most consistently successful businessmen in the country. Harry single-handedly introduced and guided me into and through the insurance industry in America, an industry I still have a significant involvement with. The top people in the top insurance companies are amongst the best and brightest this society has to offer. It is too bad that the industry is currently taking a beating as a result of the actions of a few irresponsible individuals.

Through Harry I met Bob Kerrigan, general agent for Northwestern Mutual in Los Angeles. I worked with Bob for years when he was Harry's Chief Operating Officer, and then helped Bob

with transition of his professional and personal life to Los Angeles,
three years ago. Few people in business have achieved the level of suc-
cess and sophistication, at as early an age, as has Bob. His ability to
absorb information, fully integrate it into his experience base, and then
almost immediately use it to help others grow and change, is unparal-
leled in my life. I will be forever grateful to Bob for providing me, over
the years, with the opportunity to develop pioneering ways to work
with people in business organizations. That, plus Bob's friendship, has
truly been a gift.

A number of other individuals in the insurance industry have
been extraordinarily helpful to me in focusing and expanding my pro-
fessional life. Steve Mellinger, who was Bob Kerrigan's predecessor in
Los Angeles, helped further my experience and knowledge base in the
industry and was a key factor in networking me on the west coast.

Mel Hebert, who was formerly branch manager for Manulife
Financial's office in Woodland Hills, California, was instrumental in
connecting me with the corporate offices of Manulife in Toronto.
Gord Wilson, formerly with the home office of Manulife, spearhead-
ed the introduction of High Risk Management into the organization.
As a result of my early involvement with Manulife, I met Karen
Hayward, who has played a significant role in management training
and development in the U.S. division. Few people take to heart the idea
of accountability, like Karen. Over the past few years she has nudged,
prodded, and demanded that I get my thinking and material organized
and structured, and for that caring I am indebted to her. Through
Manulife I met Jim Blackburn, formerly branch manager in
Cleveland, and now an internal consultant to the company, working to
help them implement their re-engineering strategy with the field distri-
bution system. No one synthesizes material as effectively as Jim, and
few understand and practice leadership as well.

During the past couple of years, two people – John Bond and
Colleena Sabia – have been very impactful on my life. In a relatively
short period of time, John and I have become partners in a rapidly
growing international change management consulting firm, whose
reception in the marketplace has far exceeded my expectations. John
has had a highly successful career transition organization with offices
throughout Canada, and his business savvy and acumen have been

invaluable to me. John has taught me how to grow a business, as opposed to working in one.

Colleena (who happens to be John's wife), has played a pro-found role in the development of INSITE and, in particular, has been the key driving force in literally transforming my concepts, thoughts, and outlines into a coherent whole called "High Risk Management." The book in its current form would not have been possible without Colleena's talent for seeing what concepts should look like on paper. To me, her talent is absolutely magical. I do not have a clue as to how she does it, but I love her dearly for it.

Over the years, a few key personal relationships have been very important to and very supportive of me. One of those has been the relationship with Peg English, a friend for almost twenty years. Peg was the first person to see the spark ignite between my wife, Arleah, and I, and has shared many of the key moments of our lives with us. She is one of the few people who has consistently witnessed the evolution of my personal and professional life over the last two decades, and who has been unwaveringly supportive of each and every moment.

The other person is my wife, Arleah. To say that she has believed in me and been supportive would be to trivialize her meaning in my life. She has not just hung in there through difficult times; she has insisted that I pursue my vision; that I stay on the cutting edge even when the pressures to back off reached the heights of intensity. Her commitment to her own growth and development is no less strenuous. I have never met anyone who goes after herself as much and is as true to the internal self. Her insights into people and her intuitive assessments of individuals are staggering in their speed and accuracy. Those insights and her deep caring and commitment have been nothing short of inspirational for me and our children.

INDEX

A

Acceptance
  characteristics of, 125
  of grief, 125-26
Accountability, 85, 96
  clarification of areas for, 159-60
  and deadlines, 162-64
  and expectations, 160-62
  and individuals, 158-59
  modeling by management, 166-67
  and positive and negative conse-
    quences, 164-65
  test for, 167
  value of, 157-58
Adolescent-like workers management
    of, 151-52, 154-55 problems of,
    146-47 structuring environment
    for, 150-51
Adults
  developmental stages of, 149-50
  value-confluence of, 153
Anger
  and assertion, 199
  characteristics of, 118-19
  co-opting, effects on, 201
  dysfunctional response to, 197
  expressing anger, 198
  and getting results, 199
  and grief, 118-20
  and hope trips, 201-2
  intimidation, effects on, 200
  overcoming, 119-20
  plan for healthy expression of, 202-
    4
  positive aspects of, 195
  roots of, 195
  shutting down of, 196-97, 200-202
  transforming into productivity, 204-5
Arrogance, and anger, 119
Assertion, 199
Autocratic model, conflict management,
    19091
Autonomy
  fostering autonomy, 223-25
  and high risk people, 80

versus security, 80
shift from independence to, 219-21

B

Bargaining
  and grief, 120-23
  overcoming, 122-23
  and relationships, 120-22
Behavioral model, conflict manage-
    ment, 18990 Blind loyalty, 207-9
Boundaries
  defining limits, 186-87
  success and loss of, 108-9

C

Caring, 18-21
  compared to caretaking, 18, 19, 66
  caretaking traits, 20
  development of caring mechanisms,
    20-21
  meaning of, 18
CEOs, 81
Change
  changing attitudes about change,
    23-24
  and decisions, 52-53
  and individual choice, 21-23
  and information, 54
  preparation for, 57
  and specific instructions, 161-62
Choice
  and decisions, 49-52
  and information, 47-49
  taking ownership of, 187-88
Chopra, Depak, 45
Common sense, lack of, 146-47
Communication
  during interviews, 73-74
  and relationship-building, 72-74
Competition, 85
  and information, 38-39